ID0983875

BRITISH POETRY OF THE SECOND WORLD WAR

BRITISH POETRY OF THE SECOND WORLD WAR

Linda M. Shires

St. Martin's Press   New York

All rights reserved. For information, write:
St. Martin's Press, Inc., 175 Fifth Avenue, New York, NY 10010
Printed in Hong Kong
Published in the United Kingdom by The Macmillan Press Ltd.
First published in the United States of America in 1985

ISBN 0–312–10416–2

Library of Congress Cataloging in Publication Data

Shires, Linda M., 1950–
    British poetry of the Second World War.

    Bibliography: p.
    Includes index.
    1. English poetry—20th century—History and
criticism. 2. World War, 1939–1945—Literature
and the war. 3. War poetry, English—History and
criticism. I. Title.
PR605.W66S53 1985   821′.912′09   84–15133
ISBN 0–312–10416–2

For Helen E. Shires
and
in memory of Philip M. Shires

Contents

Illustrations

Acknowledgements

My indebtedness to others is wide and deep. Without a Harold W. Dodds Fellowship and travel grants from Princeton University, I could not have begun the research necessary for this book. I owe warm thanks to the Reference Department and Rare Books Division of the Princeton University Firestone Library and to staffs of the following collections: The British Library, the Bodleian Library, and the University of London Periodicals Division.

I would like to thank the following Oxford scholars for their excellent advice: Christopher Butler, Valentine Cunningham and Lyndall Gordon. Among the British poets and editors who so kindly gave of their time to meet with me, I owe the greatest debts to: Dannie Abse, the late G. S. Fraser, Roy Fuller, John Lehmann, Michael Meyer, Peter Porter, Howard Sergeant, John Heath-Stubbs and Julian Symons. For answering specific inquiries, I would like to express appreciation to Roger Bowen of the University of Arizona, Gordon Phillips of the (London) *Times* archives, John Gross, then Editor of the *Times Literary Supplement*, Donald Davie, Philip Larkin, Gavin Ewart and Derek Stanford.

Samuel P. Hynes and A. Walton Litz of Princeton University carefully read this manuscript at various stages of its growth and offered invaluable suggestions for its improvement.

I am happy to have the opportunity to thank a group of scholars and friends who showed continued interest in the progress of this book and whose generosity proved extraordinary: Steven Cohan, Jean Howard, Anne Leugers, Katherine Oakley, Mark Patterson, Katrina Wingfield and Constance Wright. In addition to the great debt to my parents, which I acknowledge in the dedication, I am chiefly indebted to U. C. Knoepflmacher, who stood beside me from the beginning.

A generous grant from the University Senate Research Committee of Syracuse University aided me in the last stages of this project. To Marilyn Walden in Princeton and to Jean Rice in

Syracuse – my sincere thanks for the final preparation of the manuscript. Finally, the editorial pains taken by Julia Steward have made it a privilege to work with Macmillan.

L.M.S.

Grateful acknowledgement is made for permission to quote from the following copyright sources: from *Brides of Reason* by Donald Davie, by permission of the author; from manuscript materials (Add. MSS 53773, 53774, 56355, 57977) by Keith Douglas, by permission of the British Library Board; from *The Complete Poems of Keith Douglas*, edited by Desmond Graham (1978), copyright © Marie J. Douglas 1978, reprinted by permission of Oxford University Press; from *Alamein to Zem Zem* (1979) by Keith Douglas, by permission of Oxford University Press; from *Keith Douglas, A Biography* by Desmond Graham (1974), by permission of Oxford University Press; from 'Poets in this War' by Keith Douglas, by permission of J. C. Hall; statements by Gavin Ewart from *The Poetry of War 1939–1945*, edited by Ian Hamilton and Alan Ross and from *The War Poets* by Oscar Williams, by permission of Gavin Ewart; from 'Dylan Thomas' in *Essays on Twentieth Century Poets* by G. S. Fraser and from the following works by the same author: *Leaves Without a Tree*, *The Modern Writer and his World*, 'Passages from a Cairo Notebook' in *Leaves from the Storm*, 'The Poet and His Medium' in *The Craft of Letters*, 'Recent Verse: London and Cairo' in *Poetry London* (1944), *Springtime*, 'Toward Completeness' in *Seven* (1940), *The White Horseman*, and from an interview with Linda M. Shires, by permission of Mrs Paddy Fraser; from *Collected Poems 1936–1961* (André Deutsch), by permission of Roy Fuller; from statements by Roy Fuller in *The Poetry of War 1939–1945*, edited by Ian Hamilton and Alan Ross, and from an interview with Linda M. Shires, by permission of Roy Fuller; from *Collected Poems* (1965) by David Gascoyne, by permission of Oxford University Press; from an interview with G. B. H. Wightman in *Aquarius* (1978) by John Heath-Stubbs, from an interview with Linda M. Shires, and from 'Simile', by permission of John Heath-Stubbs; from *Collected Poems* by Sidney Keyes, ed. Michael Meyer, by permission of Routledge and

Kegan Paul PLC; from *Eight Oxford Poets* and *Minos of Crete* by
Sidney Keyes, by permission of Routledge and Kegan Paul PLC
and Michael Meyer; from letters published in *Sidney Keyes* by John
Guenther (London Magazine Editions), by permission of Alan
Ross; from *Jill* by Philip Larkin and from the following works by
the same author: *The North Ship*, 'The War Poet' in *Required
Writing: Miscellaneous Pieces 1955–1982* (first published in *The
Listener* 1963), by permission of Faber and Faber Ltd; from letter
to Linda M. Shires, 'Plymouth', and 'Portrait' (*Mandrake*), by
permission of Philip Larkin; from *I Am My Brother* by John
Lehmann and from the following works by the same author: *New
Writing 1939*, *Thrown to the Woolfs* (Weidenfeld and Nicolson and
Holt Rinehart) and from an interview with Linda M. Shires, by
permission of John Lehmann; from *Ha! Ha! Among the Trumpets* by
Alun Lewis and from the following works by the same author: *Last
Inspection and Other Stories*, *Raiders' Dawn*, and *Selected Poetry and
Prose*, by permission of George Allen & Unwin Ltd; from
statements by Michael Meyer in *The Cherwell* (1970) and in 'John
Heath-Stubbs in the Forties', in *Best Poetry of the Year 6*, edited by
Dannie Abse, and from an interview with Linda M. Shires, by
permission of Michael Meyer; from *Collected Poems* by F. T. Prince,
published by the Anvil Press Poetry, London and by The Sheep
Meadow Press, New York, copyright © F. T. Prince, 1979, by
permission of F. T. Prince and the Anvil Press Poetry; from
Introduction to Surrealism by Herbert Read, by permission of David
Higham Associates Ltd; from *A Map of Verona* by Henry Reed, by
permission of Jonathan Cape Ltd; from Preface to *New Signatures*
and Introduction to the *Faber Book of Modern Verse* by Michael
Roberts, by permission of Janet Adam-Smith; from *Auden and After*
by Francis Scarfe, by permission of Routledge and Kegan Paul
PLC; from an interview with Linda M. Shires, by permission of
Howard Sergeant; from 'Death of an Airman' and other poems in
Bernard Spencer: Collected Poems edited by Roger Bowen (1981),
by permission of Oxford University Press; from *Inside the Forties*
(Sidgwick and Jackson) by Derek Stanford, by permission of the
author; from *The Detective Story in Britain* and from *Notes from
Another Country* by Julian Symons, and from a letter to Linda M.
Shires, by permission of the author; from *Collected Poems* by Dylan
Thomas, by permission of J. M. Dent; from Dylan Thomas, *Poems
of Dylan Thomas*, copyright © 1945 by the Trustees for the
Copyrights of Dylan Thomas, reprinted by permission of New

Directions Publishing Corporation; from *The Inward Animal* by Terence Tiller, by permission of The Hogarth Press.

Grateful acknowledgement is also made for the photograph and sketches reproduced on pages 114, 128 and 134, these are reprinted from *Keith Douglas, A Biography* by Desmond Graham (1974) by kind permission of Oxford University Press and Desmond Graham.

Preface

It is hard to believe that a decade of poetry could be summarily dismissed as a blackout period for art; yet this is still the generally-held attitude towards the 1940s. A myth about this poetic period flourishing in England and America runs as follows: during the war and post-war years, it was impossible to create poems with a keen intelligence, a clear head or a direct voice. John Press has noted the common opinion of the decade as a time in which all sound poetic values were 'debauched, when fecund images proliferated in surrealistic luxurience'.[1] Coherent poetic structures were abandoned or lost in a punch-drunk Apocalyptic fervour and wartime hysteria. The 1940s have been allocated a prime spot in the literary pigeon-hole labelled 'Hallucinatory/ Third rate'. Perhaps no modern decade has been stereotyped so unfairly.

We view the 1940s through the distorted lenses of the 1950s poets and critics, many of whom were connected directly with the Movement. Their stereotype, consisting of misapprehensions that have been sustained by major critics up to this day, originally was an act of dissociation and self-assertion. According to their reduction, the only poets writing during the 1940s were Surrealists and Apocalyptics; these poets followed directly on the heels of Auden; and it was not until the Movement that genuine 'poetry' returned.

The Movement and others not associated with it directly distorted the previous decade when they chose the Apocalyptics (a group headed by Henry Treece and J. F. Hendry) and Dylan Thomas to typify the poetry of the period. The romantic Apocalyptics with their cannon and firework display of images and the inferior quality of even their best work stood out as a prime target. Yet no single group, and least of all this one, could be called representative of the 1940s. Furthermore, when they dismissed all poets of the 1940s along with Thomas as 'romantic scribblers',[2] they ignored the best poets of the war years who

xiii

deserve re-evaluation. Poets such as Henry Reed, Roy Fuller, G. S. Fraser, Keith Douglas and Alun Lewis hardly fit the label of wild irrationalists.

There has been a general reluctance to examine this decade seriously. Rather, the clichés about the 1940s have been maintained by critics decades later. In his influential essay 'Beyond the Gentility Principle',[3] A. Alvarez reduces the poetry of the 1940s to a reaction against the 1930s. In his over-simplification, he sees the intelligent socio-political poetry of W. H. Auden simply replaced by the disjointed ramblings of Dylan Thomas. His opinions would have been more persuasive if he had dealt with and dismissed the variety of poetic voices or more forcefully illustrated their weaknesses in light of strengths. Instead, he downgrades the decade as a time when poets, for the most part, 'kiss meaning goodbye'.

Kenneth Allott too, in his *Penguin Book of Contemporary Verse* (1950/62), falsely represents the 1940s. Allott's death in 1973 forbade any more revisions of text or introduction; yet the publishers let Allott's 1950 edition stand unchanged for twelve years until they reprinted the volume with revisions. In 1962 Allott frankly admitted his preference for Graves, Eliot, Auden, Yeats, Larkin and Davie. He declared that if he had had more space, he would have included additional poems of Davie, Larkin, Kinsella, Gunn, Tomlinson, Amis and Hughes. It is significant that in this list of would-be inclusions, there is no important figure from the forties. It seems odd that Keith Douglas, the best of the Second World War poets, finds no place here.

The fifties poets and critics and others prolonging the acceptance of a forties myth actually concentrated on the quantity of bad poetry written then. Or, even more narrowly, they chose the poetry of 1945–50 as representative; but there are two distinct periods in the decade, war and post-war, which should not be confused. This decade had the peculiar distinction of seeing a generation of poets split in half by cultural crisis instead of welded together by external events. Thus the Movement poets – Philip Larkin, John Wain, Donald Davie, Elizabeth Jennings and others – who were born in the same years as the major war poets flowered not in the 1940s but in the early 1950s. In between the departure of W. H. Auden from England and the publicity campaign of the Movement in the early fifties, the schoolfellows of Larkin, Wain and Davie turned towards a war they could not escape. After the war, social readjustment, paper shortages, and a general intellectual depression shifted attention to an older generation of poets. In the years from 1945–50, Kathleen Raine, Vernon Watkins, George Barker and others regained prominence. Their metaphysical and religious poetry is often erroneously linked with the Apocalyptics who flourished in the 1930s and early 1940s while the poets of World War Two remain ignored.

At a time when the poet's personal identity was severely threatened, when fables and myths were helpless against the reality of Nazi armies and gas chambers, there were poets who remained articulate and careful observers. Thirties poetry has been praised for its objectivity, but the early forties poetry can boast of an objectivity as well. G. S. Fraser, for instance, based in Cairo, writes of his English home and his adopted country with lucid concreteness. His personal landscapes are rooted in facts. The best poetry of the period did not succumb to ornamental falsity, but is characterized by intellectual honesty in the face of disaster and depression. Henry Reed wrote the epigraph for this generation of poets: 'Things may not be the same again; and we must fight / Not in the hope of winning but rather of keeping something alive.'

This study views the 1940s historically and concentrates on the younger generation. I do not chart the development or divergent paths of the Auden group: Day Lewis, Spender, MacNeice and Auden. I do not underestimate Auden's influence on British poetry after 1939, but it is not part of my subject. Nor do I emphasize the work of older poets such as Robert Graves or T. S. Eliot. Edith Sitwell, also of an older generation, does not find space here, nor do I treat the period of 1945–50 extensively. I mention it as background to a brief discussion of the Movement's success. My primary concern has been to reconstruct the early forties – its moods and themes – and to discover the various voices and idioms which made up the poetry scene at home and abroad. I have been interested in emphasizing the problem of order and disorder in the poet's world and in his creations during a time of crisis and in exploring the influence of war on post-war poetry.

I would like to add a word about terminology. There was a persistent habit among poets and critics during the 1940s and 1950s of using *romantic* and *Romantic* interchangeably. Most often they are referring to a special temper of mind in which emotion or imagination seems to triumph over formal considerations, not to the Romantic movement of the nineteenth century. Similarly, when they refer to *metaphysical*, they generally mean speculative or philosophically-oriented poetry, not specifically the Metaphysical poetry of the seventeenth century. I have followed them in their use of this terminology.

NOTES

1. John Press, *A Map of Modern English Verse* (London: Oxford University Press, 1969) p. 230.
2. John Wain, 'Ambiguous Gifts', *Penguin New Writing* 40 (1950) p. 127.
3. A. Alvarez, 'Beyond the Gentility Principle', *Beyond All This Fiddle* (London: Allen Lane, 1968) pp. 35–6. Also see Geoffrey Grigson, *Poetry of the Present* (London: Phoenix House, 1949) p. 23, and A. Alvarez, 'Poetry of the Fifties: in England,' International Literary Annual #1, 1958 (New York: Criterion Books, 1959) p. 98.

1 Endings and Beginnings

I

'They were all caught and caged; prisoners; watching a spectacle. Nothing happened. The tick of the machine was maddening.' So Virginia Woolf describes the members of the audience at the pageant presentation in her last novel: *Between the Acts*. The spectators represent both the stupefied British public on the eve of war watching the drama of history unfold before them, and playgoers awaiting the transformation of reality into art. Written in 1939–40 and published posthumously in 1941, *Between the Acts* is one of the finest recreations in literature of that transitional period between the 1930s and the 1940s. It captures a particular mixed mood of nostalgia, stasis, terror, and a slim hope for a future – in life or art.

In September of 1939 Virginia Woolf, like many other artists, felt herself on a voyage to nowhere. 'The Hepworths came on Monday', she recorded in her diary.[1] 'Rather like a sea voyage. Forced conversation. Boredom. All meaning has run out of everything. . . . Emptiness.' She tried on September 11 to *anchor* her mind with close work – translating Theophrastus from the original Greek. The experience of war – standing at the edge of it, living through it – was like being at sea on a raft or a liner to a surprise port, or to no port. Like the ocean itself, this widespread war meant danger and possible death as well as adventure. 'War moved', wrote Elizabeth Bowen in her novel *The Heat of the Day*, 'from the horizon to the map'; unlike World War One, it was uncontainable.[2]

It was certainly uncontainable by the old poetic formulae. And in retrospect, there is something especially dramatic about that turning-point year, 1939. By the end of the 1930s, the Auden generation had turned away from social to more personal interests. Autobiography became one of their main forms and a chief element in their work, directly as in Isherwood's *Lions and*

1

Shadows and Spender's 1939 *September Journal*, or indirectly as in the personal statements in MacNeice's *Modern Poetry* (1938).[3] At the end of the decade, these writers were concerned with ordering and structuring statements about themselves. They were preparing, in a sense, the burial tombs of their old selves. It is highly significant that, as Tolley reports, 'Nearly all the important poets of the period produced a volume of poetry in 1939 or 1940 – volumes that often had a valedictory quality, and were certainly the final collections of poetry for the thirties'.[4]

The departure of Auden and Isherwood to America in January 1939 was also symbolic of the end of an era. Auden's leaving, in particular, was resented strongly by certain members of the literary establishment who now felt abandoned by an irreplaceable leader. Yet the view that he *betrayed* his country or his fellow-poets by leaving England in time of crisis is exaggerated and unnecessarily harsh. And although it appears that the nerve of the thirties poetry went dead when Auden left, such linking is an oversimplification. Auden was not running away; he was still admired and respected by some, if not all, of the middle-class establishment. Most likely, several reasons lay behind his decision to go to the United States and settle there. He was disillusioned politically; he had lost faith in his own heroism – that is, he felt overfêted as a leader in the literary circles; and he urgently desired more privacy. America could allow him various freedoms, including greater anonymity and a more private sexual life, which England could no longer so easily provide. His poem 'September 1, 1939', written from New York City, does not proclaim retreat and defeat, as Hewison partly claims.[5] Its title bears witness to confrontation with events; its sentiments stem from disillusionment but not hopelessness; yet its wisdom is that which distance and objectivity afford. Auden does not abandon all hope, only the *clever* hopes of a decade which he feels was not intellectually honest with itself. His feelings are not those of defeat but are stronger ones – fear and anger – which prompt him to enter the fray again but with different weapons. 'I and the public know/ What all schoolchildren learn/ Those to whom evil is done/ Do evil in return.' 'We must love one another or die.' Auden eventually cut the eighth stanza from the text, a stanza which defines the *lie* of a morally and intellectually dishonest generation:

The romantic lie in the brain
Of the sensual Man-in-the-street,
The lie of Authority
Whose buildings grope the sky;
There is no such thing as the State
And no one exists alone;
Hunger allows no choice
To the citizen or the police,
We must love one another or die.

Dismissing Authority, State, and class structures, Auden terms the beliefs of his generation lies. The Second World War, in his view, was engendered to punish mankind for moral blindness in the politically-oriented thirties. Not only does Auden shift his allegiance to individual morality, but he also gives final warning to the society he once hoped to change. In a society harbouring good and evil elements, he says, men must compromise to find common boundaries. Society must unite in this way or it will fall into anarchy; the poet will now help to 'Undo the folded lie', but he will not be actively engaged politically.

The growing loss of faith in a thirties idealism; the deaths of two brilliant men in 1939, Yeats and Freud; the war in Spain and the mounting power of Hitler and Mussolini; the pessimistic sense of failure which crept into the consciousness of the general public; Auden's and Isherwood's departure; the declaration of war in autumn, 1939 – all these facts create an overwhelming sense of an ending. One of the briefer obituaries to the greatest hopes of the thirties poets was written by Randall Swingler in *Our Time* (May 1941). There he hoisted the coffin of the Auden generation into the grave:

The war has put an end to that literary generation. All their fantasies have been outdone by the reality. Auden's conspiracies, legendary plots, amazing assaults upon social life, look silly and childish now before the blatant conspiracies and villainies of real politics. Nothing is left of their imaginings but the twilight, peopled by the ghosts of literary values long defunct. . . .

Perhaps the strongest statement in support of this sealing off of the thirties is made in MacNeice's introduction to his *Collected Poems*

1925–1940 where he wrote: 'When a man collects his poems, people think him dead. I am collecting mine not because I am dead, but because my past life is. Like most other people in the British Isles I have little idea what will happen next – I shall go on writing, but my writing will presumably be different'.

MacNeice entertained some hope for the future in 1939, but most other members of the literary establishment did not. At the end of the thirties, creative writers gravely doubted the future of literature – editors too believed that they were witnessing the dissolution of an entire civilization. In January 1939, T. S. Eliot terminated his editorship of *The Criterion*. In his editorial 'Last Words' (volume XVIII, no. LXXI), he described what his aims had been in this periodical, how its contents had reflected the changing times. In addition, he revealed that for several years he had been confused about the future of Britain. He referred to his commentaries which bore painful witness to 'the grave dangers to this country which might result from the lack of any vital political philosophy, either explicit or implicit'. Further, Eliot considered the problematic future of literary magazines. He cited the series of articles 'Present Discontents' from the *TLS* – articles on the state of reviewing which reflected apprehension about a decline in literacy. He wrote:

> I would refer the reader to 'Present Discontents' (now reprinted as a pamphlet) for a survey of some of the specifically literary symptoms of decline. For they are only symptoms; they cannot be treated by themselves; the demoralization of society goes very much deeper. Even the terms used by those who are to some extent conscious of this demoralization are sometimes alarming. . . . As the state of arts and letters is a symptom of decline, so it might be a symptom of a true revival. But in any case, the immediate future is not bright.

Eliot's personal loss of commitment is extreme:

> In the present state of public affairs – which has induced in myself a depression of spirits so different from any other experience of fifty years as to be a new emotion – I no longer feel the enthusiasm necessary to make a literary review what it should be. This is not to suggest that I consider literature to be at this time, or at any time, a matter of indifference. On the

contrary, I feel that it is all the more essential that authors who are concerned with that small part of 'literature' which is really creative – and seldom immediately popular – should apply themselves sedulously to their work. . . .[6]

And yet writers of all ages had lost inspiration to go on with their work. Stephen Spender, suffering a private loss as war broke out, recorded his stifled creative self in his *September Journal*: 'I feel as if I could not write again. Words seem to break in my mind like sticks when I put them down on paper. I cannot see how to spell some of them. Sentences are covered with leaves. . . '.[7] The younger Stefan Schimanski recorded in May 1940: 'Life suddenly seemed to have come to an end by an invisible power'.[8] 'Wariness had driven away poetry', wrote Elizabeth Bowen of wartime England in *The Heat of the Day*, 'from hesitating to feel came the time when you no longer could'. In an article in *The New Statesman* (23 May 1942) Bowen, then in her forty-third year, referred directly to the dilemma facing all creative artists in these years: 'There is at present evident, in the reflective writer, not so much inhibition or dulling of his own feeling as an inability to obtain the focus necessary for art. One cannot reflect, or reflect on, what is not wholly in view. These years rebuff the imagination as much by being fragmentary as by being violent.' The imagination could no longer dominate and transform events, but only register aspects of the surrounding scene. This lack of inspiration and structures to order impressions reinforced a disbelief in 'culture'. 'There is such a doubt about the continuity of civilization', wrote Orwell in his London letter of 3 January 1941 (*Partisan Review*), 'as can hardly have existed for hundreds of years, and meanwhile there are the air raids, which make continuous intellectual life very difficult'.[9] 'This is not a writer's world', suggested Orwell. '1939 was not a year in which to start a literary career', said Forster in a poetry review in *The Listener* (11 January 1940).

II

The problems for the poet in wartime were exactly those which Virginia Woolf exposed mercilessly and brilliantly in *Between the Acts*: a new uncertainty about the role of art, a loss of inspiration in the face of violence, and the search for a new style to capture the sense of crisis. Young poets of the war era could no longer accept the tone, idiom and interests of the Auden generation. For the poets who made their reputations in the forties were responding to their literary forefathers – in mimicry and in defiance – as well as to their own historical time.

To set the stage for the forties poets, I would like to review briefly some main points about the poetry of the thirties. One of the central interests of the Auden generation was heroism. All generations require heroes of some sort, but there seemed to be a special need in the thirties to move away from the anti-hero of the twenties. The older definition of hero-as-warrior had been fully exploded in the trenches of the First World War. Yet the poets of the 1930s sought such heroes again.

While Isherwood ironically found his leader in a man called Upward, most of the literary left found their great man in Auden. Auden gained poetic leadership largely through his ability to make structures of belief in parable form and his adoption of a new versatile 'language of action' for poetry. In his early poems, one can see his new images, in fact a wholly new 'other country'. The old world is Yeats' sick and dying animal transformed to derelict machinery and rusting rail lines. The new country beckons. Journeys to borders, to unknown frontiers, are daring ventures. In an age of no positive heroes, travellers, mountain climbers, airmen – all who risked themselves for a cause or on a dare, whether successful or not – are heroic. They act, and in moving away from a dying society and world, they affirm themselves, and set examples for others. Of course these modes of action are 1930s substitutes for choosing to go to war or undertaking dangerous personal missions in battle, the older modes of effort and glory. But Spender's poem 'I Think Continually of Those Who Were Truly Great' is more than elegy. The truly great are indeed gone, but they inspire the 1930s idealist to make an effort on his own. Even if only by writing, a substitute for action, he may somehow matter and affect external events. Out of a dying nation, Auden drew forth a wellspring of hope, a wellspring whose source was in earlier and older certainties.

These men of the thirties must have looked upon themselves as essentially weak men or as outsiders. In the face of overshadowing historical events, they tried to make themselves and each other into heroes. They felt that by changing themselves into 'stronger' men, they would become more than survivors. So they emulated an artist like Auden who had fresh ideas and appeared sure of himself, and others such as T. E. Lawrence. In Lawrence, they could see an image of their present selves: weak, neurotic, writer, and outsider. In him they could also see one who had made a successful self-transformation. Auden himself viewed Lawrence as a symbolic figure. In 'T. E. Lawrence', *Now and Then* (Spring 1934), Auden wrote: 'To me Lawrence's life is an allegory of the transformation of the truly Weak man into the Truly Strong Man, an answer to the question "How shall the self-conscious man be saved?" and the moral seems to be this: "self-consciousness is an asset, in fact the only friend of our progress".' Lawrence was the inspiration for such figures as the airman in *The Orators*. As they made heroes of Auden and T. E. Lawrence, so the thirties poets made heroes of themselves.

But as the political realities fearfully worsened, a confidence in mankind which the Auden group had attempted to revive began to dim. In July 1936, war broke out in Spain. Some writers, acting on their political beliefs, went to Spain, fought and died there. For those who stayed at home, including Day Lewis, or went later in 1937, such as MacNeice, Spender and Auden, the war testified to a society morally diseased. Now the whole future of Europe lay in the balance. The poets' mood and the nation's general consciousness had become darker – the forces of good were not able to be so clearly distinguished from those of evil. In the last year of peace, as Hitler moved against Austria, politics turned from propaganda to reality.

But the political crisis in Europe only speeded a literary reaction which had started beforehand. No retrospection will take us to the true beginning or end of any cultural movement. Yet it is important to note that in spite of Auden's popularity and devoted following in 1939, some contemporaries openly criticized his mode before the war. This thirties reaction against Audenesque poetry came, however, not only from his contemporaries. The older literary establishment as well, and especially the new generation revolted against what they saw as a conglomerate of politics and psychology in poetry.

One example of a mixed critical response to Auden is the *New Verse* tribute to him, a double number of 1937. For this issue, Geoffrey Grigson requested comments and essays from Auden's associates and from other poets outside of his circle. His friends wrote glowing tributes. His champion Grigson hailed him as a genius. But admiring remarks from other contributors were qualified. George Barker liked Auden's work because 'it exhilarates me in a way which height, ozone, speed, love, drink, and violent exercise do not: I mean it has the singular effect of poetry upon my senses. I dislike aspects of it because behind or through the poetry I discern a clumsy interrogative finger questioning me about my matriculation certificate, my antecedents and my annual income.' Frederic Prokosch was even more critical: 'There is something a bit wrong about it all, I suspect: and he knows it: the feelings of guilt, of withdrawal, of self-pity, of hysteria, creep in. There are technical dangers too – glibness, theatricality, cocksureness, opportunism, laziness – to put it harshly.' Dylan Thomas had this to say: 'I sometimes think of Mr Auden's poetry as a hygiene, a knowledge and practice, based on a brilliantly prejudiced analysis of contemporary disorders, relating to the preservation and promotion of health, a sanitary science and flushed of melancholies. I sometimes think of his poetry as a great war, admire intensely the mature, religious, and logical fighter, and deprecate the boy bushranger.' Several contributors remarked on a lack of development, even a regression in technique: Charles Madge, Auden's contemporary, considered his style's 'immature quality' – once 'an attraction', he wrote, it 'becomes an embarrassment'. The much older Herbert Read saw 'a definite backsliding in the technique of verse'. And Ezra Pound characteristically replied by suggesting that other poets of the time would be worth Grigson's consideration instead of his fêting Auden at so young an age. 'I might be inclinde to answer yr not IF I cd. discover why your little lot neglects to import cumming; W.C.W. and one or two other items of interest.' (*sic*)

Much earlier, in 1932, and just as the Auden group was being recognized as the new voice in poetry, Virginia Woolf criticized them in her pamphlet *Letter to A Young Poet*. She did not like the absence of 'real' human characters and an ordinary universe in their poetry. She attacked them for having neither 'eyes nor ears', for having a tone too near despair. She found Spender *unintelligible*. For the duration of the decade, she disapproved of their poetry and she damned them again, eight years later in 1940, in her essay 'The Leaning Tower', a lecture delivered in Brighton and published in *Folios of New Writing* by John Lehmann in that autumn.

In fact, though, the direction of the Auden group did not

remain the same between 1932 and 1940. Their faith in political activity had declined alongside a burgeoning interest in other structures of belief. One can note this shift of focus by examining the prefaces of their chief promoter, Michael Roberts. Roberts had edited the first collection of their work: *New Signatures* in 1931. In the preface, he helped to define the mood of this (then) new generation. Compelled to say something of their political ties, he fell into vague and brief remarks: 'It is natural that the recognition of the importance of others should sometimes lead to what appears to be the essence of the communist attitude: the recognition that oneself is no more important than a flower in a field; that it may be good to sacrifice one's own welfare that others may benefit; to plough in this year's crop so that next year's may benefit: the return is certain, what matters is who receives it.' Roberts' statement of political affiliation is actually nothing more than a sense of old boy neighbourliness. But, as Samuel Hynes notes, many of the poems of *New Signatures* are political in that they acknowledge a political reality which Roberts and all of his generation felt: the sense of imminent disaster, the idea of apocalypse.[10]

By the time Roberts edited the anthology *New Country*, he authoritatively assessed the state of the nation's illness and the need for a cure. He advanced the idea of revolution – in politics and in poetry. But like others of the Auden generation, by 1936 Roberts was also withdrawing from the political 'arena'. In his preface to *The Faber Book of Modern Verse*, both the language of revolution and his praise for communist poetry were quite absent. There, Roberts goes so far as to suggest that 'a too self-conscious concern with "contemporary" problems deflects the poet's effort from his true objective'.

Roberts' aversion to a literature concerned with 'contemporary problems' coincided with his new devotion to philosophical questions that had long interested him. His switch of attention was symptomatic of a general direction the Auden group would also take. Faced with the impending world crisis, MacNeice, Day Lewis, Spender and Auden realized that their politicizing had been simplistic. What was required was a 'change of heart' in individual man. These four poets did not all move from a secular to a religious centre, but certainly their common concern promoted an individual humanism.

Stephen Spender's essay *The New Realism, A Discussion*, published by the Hogarth Press in 1939, acts as a valuable summary of this common redirection. Spender here defined the only duty of the artist in wartime: 'to remain true to standards which he can discover only within himself' (p. 3). 'Far too many writers', he warned, 'have been driven away from the centre of their real interest towards some outer rim of half creating, half agitation. A great deal is said about saving culture, but the really important thing is to have a culture to save' (p. 24).

III

Whether they belonged to Auden's generation, or to the older literary establishment, like Virginia Woolf, or to groups as radical as the Surrealists and Apocalyptics, most writers in the late 1930s concurred in calling for a change of heart.

For the youngest poets, however, contributing to this change necessarily involved deposing Auden and his group. Upon first meeting John Heath-Stubbs at Oxford in 1940, Sidney Keyes criticized the Auden followers with this indictment of their leader: 'Auden is not a poet' (John Heath-Stubbs in conversation). Keyes, one of the most promising poets of the Oxford scene and soon to win a reputation as the greatest war poet of his time, was attacking Auden for his didactic tone.

By 1939, those among the younger poets who chose to wear Auden's cloak at all, wore it lightly. Drummond Allison, for instance, whose poetry is derivative from Auden, did not mind being published first in an anthology edited by the hostile Keyes. Roy Fuller, whose Audenesque postures are evident in his first book of poetry, published in 1939, has admitted Auden's influence on him. But he called his first volume 'imitative, yet without a *dominating* influence' to bind together poems which failed to 'coalesce'.[11] No doubt, young poets wish to be dissociated as soon as possible from their masters. It is clear that this younger generation felt that their response to the world would have to be very different from that of their elders. A little known poet of the time, Donald Bain, was explicit in his rejection of earlier poetry. He writes in 'War Poet',

We only watch, and indicate and make our
    scribbled pencil notes,
We do not wish to moralize, only to ease
    our dusty throats.

Artists like Bain were forced to reject a poetry rendering
universal response such as poets had attempted in earlier political
crises. With no possibility of writing a poetry of propaganda,
warning, compassion, horror or militarism – or any easy wedding
of such attitudes, the poets of the Second World War resorted to
simply recording and to accepting a range of conflicting
responses. Like other poets, Bain surmises that perhaps time will
afford an older self or a new generation of poets to determine the
centrally important. But for the present, he accepts everything
equally, and records all. He simply does not have distance enough
from the scene, he feels, to place value. The years 1939–42,
beginning with the 'phoney war' of 1939–40, actually encouraged
both introspection and a non-judgmental observance of the
outward scene. For Bain and for his fellows, the old metaphors
and symbols were no longer functional without alteration. There
was no journey to a new life now, no mountain to ascend, no
jigsaw pieces to put together for meaning.

While the major metaphor of the thirties had been the journey,
now that war was here, the voyage metaphor continued but
strangely modified. The young poets typically rejected any type of
successful Audenesque journeys.[12] Sidney Keyes, for instance,
held out little hope of finding anything but death at the end of his
voyage. In 'Advice for a Journey', he writes:

The drums mutter for war and soon we must begin
To seek the country where they say that joy
Springs flowerlike among the rocks, to win
The fabulous golden mountain of our peace.

Yet Keyes knows that joy is as elusive as peace. 'We are too
young', he says, to explore; we have not the skills. He concludes
his poem without illusions:

Go forth, my friends, the raven is no sibyl;
Break the clouds' anger with your unchanged faces.
You'll find, maybe, the dream under the hill –
But never Canaan, nor any golden mountain.

Roy Fuller's 1939 poem, 'The Journey' (placed first in his
Collected Poems), also depicts an aborted quest. A man travels all
day to reach a house, but as he approaches his goal, the sun sets,
frost descends and the path hardens like metal. Symbols on the
gatepost warn ominously:

> On the gate-posts he saw a carven shield,
>   On each gate the same symbol,
> A shield with a carven deathshead in stone.
>   His feet began to stumble.

The last stanza renders the epitaph of a man deluded by heroic
tales of an outmoded past. He is lured unknowingly to death:

> In his cracking brain, his tortured thews,
>   A little world is burning:
> The snow, the treading rooks, the plan
>   Of a last mistaken journey.

Other writers used the metaphor of the journey and transformed it by connecting it with water.[13] There is an hallucinatory
or dream-like quality to this mysterious water 'journey to
nowhere', a metaphor that captures well the mood of those early
years of war. From the vantage point of 1948, Geoffrey Grigson
looked back and remarked in *Poetry of the Present* that the quality of
daily life which he best remembered was that of rush and
change.[14] There was a constant 'loss of equilibrium'. He uses the
metaphor of a raft being tipped over repeatedly and then righted
by the waves. John Lehmann's perceptions of the early war years
are found in the first volume of his autobiography, *I Am My
Brother*.[15] It was, he recorded, 'as if our whole civilization was a
giant liner that had left its berth and was slowly sailing into
unknown waters under a thickening fog. . .'. He noted 'the
strangeness of the journey we were embarked upon'. It was no
longer a journey to an allegorical mountain peak, or to war – to the
crisis which had long been coming – but a journey to stillness, to
peace or to death.

'Embarkation Song', a war poem by Geoffrey Matthews, is
written as a personal statement but also for his contemporaries
who faced early military service. Although it describes a troopship
manoeuvre, the poem also narrates a voyage into the oppressive,

semi-mythical unknown. Matthews describes the water around him as 'Salt water beside me, an endless bay of water / Is there a way out?' Promising his sweetheart not to ask her whereabouts when he is gone, he queries: 'But quick, tell me once more why I am going, / Before it is too late.' This journey was not by choice. The reasons for 'going' were not understood and inevitably, the voyagers felt helpless.

Alun Lewis, who was to die on active duty in Burma in 1944 in circumstances which remain mysterious, used the image of a water journey as a starting point for several memorable poems.[16] He developed the double vision hinted at by Matthews, a vision including the woman left behind. Yet when Lewis writes of his pregnant wife and her unborn child in his poem of leavetaking, 'On Embarkation', he also bids farewell to his own potential creativity apart from the world of war:

> The steel bows break, the churning screw burns white.
> Each pallid face wears an unconscious smile.
> And I – I pray my unborn tiny child
> Has five good senses and an earth as kind
> As the sweet breast of her who gives him milk
> And waves me down this first clandestine mile.

In 'Song', he concentrates on one half of the self-division apparent in line 120 of 'On Embarkation': 'I – I'. As he sees dead bodies floating off the Cape, Lewis imagines himself as one of them and writes the lamenting song of his wife. As the survivor left at home, she too is 'lost among the waves' and 'rolled / Helpless in the sea' as 'Cell by cell the coral reef / Builds an eternity of grief'.

For many poets, water and the water journey became more closely identified with a chosen death. In 'Water Music' Lewis describes a singing voice at the heart of a lake, the lake and music he will later use metaphorically for his own soul. Urging total involvement in the dark and unknown, the voice prompts him to embark on that final journey towards the cold unknown realm of death:

> Cold is the lake water
> And dark as history
> Hurry and fear not
> This oldest mystery.

This strange voice singing,
This slow deep drag of the lake,
This yearning, yearning, this ending
Of the heart and its ache.

IV

In the May 1939 issue of *New Verse*, the closing of Eliot's *Criterion*
and the death of *The London Mercury* were noted. Not only were old
metaphors dead, but the old forums were closing. *New Verse*,
which itself had come into existence because of Auden, did not
return after May 1939. It was an unexpected end since the April
issue began a 'new series'. But in May, Grigson realized that the
time for *New Verse* was over. In his last issue he wrote a review of
Auden's *In Time of War*. It is a tribute to Auden, an elegy for what
Grigson felt was best in the thirties, and a pessimistic prophecy for
the future of art. He wrote:

> . . . there are many people who might quote of Auden: 'To you I
> owe the first development of my imagination; to you I owe the
> withdrawing of my mind from the low brutal part of my nature
> to the lofty, the pure, and the perpetual.' Auden is now clear,
> absolutely clear, of foolish journalists, Cambridge detractors
> and envious creepers and crawlers of party and Catholic
> reaction and the new crop of loony and eccentric small
> magazines in England and America. He is something good and
> creative in European life in a time of the very greatest evil.[17]

Twentieth Century Verse, edited by Julian Symons and, like *New
Verse*, dedicated to a certain 'sane' set of values, also shut up shop
in 1939. During the three years of its existence such notables as
Roy Fuller, Gavin Ewart, D. S. Savage, H. B. Mallalieu, Ruthven
Todd and Wallace Stevens had appeared as contributors. In 1939
a future was questionable.

Before war was declared, Mr Symons and Mr Grigson met for
two lunches at the Café Royal to discuss the possibility of joining
forces on a new magazine.[18] Their editorial policies were not
irreconcilable, and it seemed advantageous to unite. Both were
feeling the financial strain imposed by running a little magazine
alone. In his memoir *Notes from Another Country*, Julian Symons

recalled the meetings. 'I can't now remember just what course the conversations took, but I do recall that Geoffrey was eager to look at my subscription list so that he could see how far it coincided with that of *New Verse*, and that I was reluctant to reveal it.'[19] Symons also recalled that Grigson wished to edit the new magazine and make Symons his assistant. But ultimately, another factor proved more important in ending discussions about a new magazine. In a recent letter Mr Symons explained: 'What's interesting is how strongly we both felt the war was coming and would change things; then when it came both thought (wrongly) that it would mean the end of little magazines; although we were right in thinking that there wouldn't be much poetry printed that either of us cared about'.[20]

The most important magazine casualties of 1939 were *The Criterion*, *The London Mercury*, *Twentieth Century Verse* and *New Verse*. The folding of these important forums and the uncertainty felt by literary editors in London concerning any new projects did not alone signal an ending. For as a public literary arena narrowed, the writer too lost a community to compose for and to test himself against.

Paradoxically though, as war approached, public demand for literature increased. A trend toward serious reading – the classic English novels, Milton, religious poetry of the past – eventually broadened out to include contemporary works. In 1935, Allen Lane had first issued Penguin paperbacks and soon moved by popular demand from a line of reprints of bestsellers to new titles and more serious educational and political books. In spite of the paper shortage, book sales increased 50 per cent from 1938–44.[21] The blitzing of libraries increased demand; so did the blackout. The people called for more poetry and reprints of classics. Such a market actually helped the young writer to get published. Stephen Spender recalled that 'even less known poets could reckon their sales as between two and four thousand instead of in the hundreds, as would have been the case before the war'.[22]

In the light of this need for reading material and the decrease in paper supply, it was perhaps inevitable that new literary magazines would flourish even though older ones collapsed. It is in the nature of the little magazines, writes Ian Hamilton, to believe that no one else can do what it is doing. 'Each magazine needs a new decade and each decade needs a new magazine.'[23]

One of the new magazines of 1939, and the one most people

associate with the decade of the forties, was Cyril Connolly's *Horizon*. Connolly started *Horizon* in September and published it from Stephen Spender's flat in Lansdowne Terrace. Compared with other magazines such as *The Criterion* or *New Verse*, *Horizon* was creatively cautious, even timid. Connolly's manifesto had declared: 'A magazine should be the reflection of its time, and one that ceases to reflect this should come to an end'. Feeling that the contents were too tame, subscribers reacted negatively to *Horizon's* first issue. They complained that it offered nothing 'new'. Throughout the issues of *Horizon*, Connolly held on to a past he felt was disintegrating in preference to abandoning himself completely to the present. The past he sought to protect was tied up closely with a sense of English tradition and with the European achievement in arts and letters. Declaring to readers that his job was to keep traditions alive, Connolly consistently lamented the huge gap he saw between culture and real life. In the course of the decade, he did remind them of a civilization worth saving and eagerly printed the ideas of such Europeans as Cavafy, Éluard, Malraux, Bartok and Picasso.

Behind Connolly's credo (stated in the first issue of *Horizon*) lay a severe disappointment with politics: 'Our standards are aesthetic, and our politics are in abeyance'. And to some degree, the magazine steadily wrote elegies for the thirties generation. Connolly saw the civilization he loved fall ill and be consigned to the hospital operating table – 'we sit in the waiting room'. Looking through a run of *Horizon* now, one has a distinct feeling of *déjà vu*. Its standard fare is not exciting. *Horizon's* conservatism is discernible in the editor's crablike movements whenever he discusses the artist's role in wartime. Connolly is torn between isolating the artist in an ivory tower away from history and allowing him the freedom to write about current events. He takes no strong permanent stand. In 1940 alone, as Ian Hamilton notes, Connolly wavered in distinct confusion through various magazine issues. He wondered what attitude to strike about war and the artist. Interestingly, his changing opinions seem to follow political events fairly accurately. In January, war was dismissed as a bore; in May, as the Germans invaded Holland and Belgium and Churchill was elected Prime Minister, Connolly viewed war as the enemy of all creative activity. In December when the British had recovered command of the Eastern Mediterranean and moved to take Egypt from the Italian forces, Connolly felt war was a necessity that had to be accommodated.

In spite of the editor's shifting opinions on the subject of the artist's role in wartime, the contents of *Horizon* do not reflect much change. Essentially Connolly's magazine remained aesthetically-oriented, but he had to rely on the last generation for a good deal of his material. In an interview in *The Listener* in 1940 he lamented the literary wasteland around him: 'As for the present, speaking as an editor, I find it a disheartening business. It is not only that so many young writers are in the Army, but that so many of the old ones seem dispirited, and I am not conscious of any particular awakening or renaissance or discovery of new forms or fresh language being made'.[24] Yet his despair at the contemporary scene only reinforced an urgency to find for literature a peaceful home.

Further, Connolly's active flirtation with self-importance diminishes his lament for a dying civilization; his elegies for culture are often weakened by a whining tone. We must grant that *Horizon*, in spite of its snobbery, fulfilled noble aims. Its main importance lay in its existence at all. At a time when other strong periodicals were closing, *Horizon* began. The despair and disgust persuading Eliot, Symons and Grigson to accept setbacks had another, quite different, effect on Connolly. In spite of the fact that *Horizon* did little for new poets, it helped keep literature before the public eye in a magazine format.

Two other magazines begun in 1939 were extremely important although they never reached the reputation of *Horizon*: *Poetry Quarterly* and *Poetry (London)*. These journals, edited respectively by Wrey Gardiner and Tambimuttu, were forums for new poets. Unlike *Horizon*, which in one issue printed no poetry at all because of Connolly's belief that there was none worth printing, these magazines encouraged the young. Derek Stanford recalled in his memoir *Inside the Forties* that the war numbers of *PQ* contained very little work of men older than thirty-five.[25]

The editorial policy of Tambimuttu, the more colourful of the two editors, was liberal in the extreme. Often mocked in the period, his indiscriminate generosity accounts for the low quality of many of the *Poetry (London)* issues. 'No man is small enough to be neglected as a poet', he wrote in *Poetry London's* first issue. 'Every healthy man is a full vessel, though vessels are of different

sizes. In a poetry magazine we can only take account of those sizes
of vessels which represent humanity as a whole.'

Tambimuttu may sound vague and histrionic in his 'First
Letter' – he was certainly not a 'common sense' editor. He can be
criticized for lacking sound principles of literary selection, but
there was also a positive side to his immense tolerance. Poets who
found a forum in *Poetry (London)* included Lawrence Durrell, D. S.
Savage, Dylan Thomas and Nicholas Moore. Nor should it be
forgotten that for all the slush he admitted, Tambimuttu also
printed some of Keith Douglas' poems and edited the first volume
of Douglas' poems.

The literary editor seeking to encourage young poets most often
was John Lehmann who, in his association with the Hogarth
Press and in his succession of 'magazines', published fresh talent
throughout the war and after. With his Christmas 1939 issue of
New Writing, a twice-yearly hardcover series printed by the
Hogarth Press, he too closed a chapter of his life, just as other
poets and editors were making endings and taking stock. 'It has
hitherto appeared every six months', he wrote, 'but that chapter
in its existence is now closed, though its readers and its
contributors can rest assured that sooner or later, in one form or
another, its work will be continued.' Lehmann incorporated this
magazine into *Folios of New Writing*, describing the result as a 'lean
war substitute'.[26] His sentiments about culture were like Connolly's but with an important difference. 'What I felt very keenly
was that the Press [Hogarth] should somehow or other keep the
flag of poetry flying – a flag that had been one of its chief
distinctions before the war, especially in the series of the Hogarth
Living Poets. If we kept that flag flying, young authors would
know that we were still interested in them.'[27] So Lehmann
recalled the early war years from a vantage point of almost forty
years.

Lehmann's persistent confidence drove him to arrange publication of a new periodical with Allen Lane: *Penguin New Writing*.
Lehmann could never really abide the ivory tower aspect of
Horizon, and promoted (through all of his many literary ventures)
encouragement of the unknown writer. The average issue of
Penguin New Writing contained much social reportage, for instance:
what it felt like to be in the navy. Readily available and easily
portable in kitbags, the magazine was the most popular literary
phenomenon of the war years. Even in mid-1943, when paper

restrictions forced the monthly to become a quarterly, every issue sold as many copies as were printed: between 75 000 and 100 000.[28] Those who felt that literature was at an end had been proved decisively wrong.

V

In *Between the Acts*, summary statement of a decade, Virginia Woolf does not ask only: will art last through such a crisis as world war? Her question is that of all the serious and dedicated artists and editors and readers who felt so pessimistic. Will art of the first quality last?

Virginia Woolf's artist figure, Miss LaTrobe, presents a pageant that distills literary and political history up to 1939. Metaphorically the village pageant represents the last English garden party; it is the ending of a way of life and of an era. It is not, however, simply an outline of history. *Between the Acts* questions the relationship between the civilized world of art and the brutal world of war and the nature of that relationship. It prepares us for the questions of British journalists of 1939 and the early 1940s: Where are the war poets? Where is the art of crisis?

Virginia Woolf has a different voice in *Between the Acts* than in her earlier fictions. The new voice which she adopts, that of an elder stateswoman, is necessary for the urgent defence of her art against history-making events. She is no longer writing coterie books like *The Waves*. Rather she is shifting from a private and introspective mode into a more public kind of writing, but she is still defending the life of the imagination. Ambition, failure, success in creative life, these topics are woven together as a leit-motiv through all of Woolf's work. Yet never before has she so seriously despaired about the creative act. Her earlier artist figures, such as Lily Briscoe, are triumphant in their visions. But Miss LaTrobe's vision is ruined.

Between the Acts records a failure of artistic conception and completion but it also tentatively queries the future of art. Miss LaTrobe feels that her play for the village has been a failure, 'another damned failure'.[29] Art has not been able to capture the reality and transform it. The artist damns the audience: 'Blood seemed to pour from her shoes. This is death, death, death, she noted in the margin of her mind; when illusion fails. Unable to lift her hand she stood facing the audience' (p. 180). Her vision is ruined by a storm and by the audience who insistently searches for and yet cannot find a 'meaning' in her pageant.

In the autumn of 1939 Virginia Woolf wrote in her journal: 'This war has begun in cold blood. One merely feels that the killing machine has to be set in action. So far the *Athenia* has been sunk. It seems entirely meaningless – a perfunctory slaughter like taking a jar in one hand, a hammer in the other. Why must this be smashed? Nobody knows . . . And all the blood has been let out of common life . . . of course all creative power is cut off.'[30] From the opening lines of her 1939 fiction – 'It was a summer's night and they were talking, in the big room with the windows open to the garden, about the cesspool' – the beautiful and the still are degraded and deflated. A hammer of events has smashed the creative spirit.

Images of violence in *Between the Acts* document this breaking spirit. They prophesy the destructive outside forces assaulting all artists of the early 1940s. As it lunges through the bushes, a playful dog becomes an eyeless monster and destroys the world of a young child. Into scenes of civilized behaviour, Woolf inserts images of terrifying power. No one can any longer escape into fictions or illusions. The newspaper has replaced the book, says Isa, for her generation. And what the newspaper details is violence. On this particular day: rape, metaphorically: the rape of the imagination. Isa reads of 'A horse with a green tail' which she considers romantic, then she reads: 'The troopers told her the horse had a green tail; but she found it was just an ordinary horse. And they dragged her up to the barrack room where she was thrown upon a bed. Then one of the troopers removed part of her clothing, and she screamed and hit him about the face.' As Isa continues to read, the door to the room opens and 'in came Mrs Swithin carrying a hammer'. A dog/monster, a story of rape, a hammer – these are just three of a host of images portraying vicious actions and cruel instruments which destroy everyday domestic scenes in the novel. But perhaps the presentation of Act IV of the pageant best summarizes this horror. It is an Act meant to represent the present time (1939). Following the entrance of figures from the League of Nations, optimistic music foretells better times ahead. But then the tune changes and the promising future is cut off: 'Snapped, broke; jagged . . . What a jungle and a jingle . . . Nothing ended. So abrupt. And corrupt. Such an outrage; such an insult' (p. 183). At this point, children run in from bushes carrying brass candlesticks, jars, mirrors, tin cans, bits of scullery glass – all sharp and jagged instruments which they hold up to the audience as reflectors. The audience sees itself: part human, part beast, broken. And yet the audience does not understand.

Miss LaTrobe, especially desiring to communicate her vision of the present, is forced to admit failure. She drinks herself into a sleepy stupor at the local pub. In the end she realizes another vision – that of a couple, but her conception is never transformed to art, and she dozes off into a welcome rest. Virginia Woolf tantalizes us at the end of her fiction with the same vision. The coda presents a couple talking, but we do not see the action she foretells: a battle and peace again.

In spite of failures and despair in *Between the Acts*, Woolf is qualifyingly hopeful about the future of art. For still alive is 'the impulse which leads us to the window at midnight to smell the bean', or 'the resolute refusal of some pimpled dirty little scrub in sandals to sell his soul'. But more important, the visionary impulse to transform, though old, lingers on. Lucy, old Mrs Swithin (whose name itself alludes to the possession of something *within*), can still find life's beauty and meaning in spite of endless savagery. 'Then she had a glimpse of silver – the great carp himself, who came to the surface so very seldom. They slid on, in and out between the stalks, silver; pink; gold; splashed; streaked; pied. "Ourselves," she murmured.' While other characters see themselves as only orts, fragments and scraps, Lucy has the faith to follow this fish, and through her vision, to see a glory in humanity.

Art, Woolf knew, could not be an agent in changing history, yet it was all that more important. As she wrote in her *Journal*, 6 September 1939: '. . . any idea is more real than any amount of war misery. . . . And the only contribution one can make – this little pitter patter of ideas – is my whiff of shot in the cause of freedom'. Woolf's challenge was not to preserve art for its own sake alone, but to keep the imagination strong against the savage and inhuman, and to produce quality art in time of crisis. In this fiction she wrote with special sensitivity of the end of a decade: 1939 – a year when the past broke off from the present, when the present itself became fragmentary, and when the future was uncertain. The challenge for the artist in *Between the Acts* is the challenge for the poets of the 1940s – for the generation born in one war and bred to die in the next.

NOTES

1. Virginia Woolf, in Leonard Woolf (ed.), *A Writer's Diary* (New York: Harcourt Brace, 1953; originally published London: The Hogarth Press, 1953) p. 305. Also see Anthony Powell's *The Valley of Bones*, *The Kindly Ones*, and *At Lady Molly's* which are set during wartime.
2. Elizabeth Bowen, *The Heat of the Day* (London: Jonathan Cape, 1949 and New York: Knopf, 1949) p. 87.
3. 'September Journal,' first appearing in *Horizon*, has been reprinted in Stephen Spender's *The Thirties and After: Poetry, Politics, People 1933–1970* (New York: Random House, 1978). See pp. 69–102. Spender has omitted five personal paragraphs in the later publication. See A. Walton Litz, 'Revising the Thirties,' *Sewanee Review*, 87 (Fall 1979) pp. 660–6.
4. A. T. Tolley, *The Poetry of the Thirties* (London: Victor Gollancz, 1975) p. 376.
5. Robert Hewison, *Under Siege* (London: Weidenfeld & Nicolson, 1977) pp. 101–2.
6. T. S. Eliot, 'Last Words', *The Criterion* XVIII, no. XXXI (January 1939) pp. 272–5. For a similar despairing tone, see Cyril Connolly, *Enemies of Promise* (London: Routledge & Kegan Paul), first edn 1938, revised edn 1949.
7. Stephen Spender, 'September Journal', *Horizon* I, no. 2 (February 1940) p. 102.
8. Stefen Schimanski, in Stefen Schimanski and Henry Treece (eds), *Leaves of the Storm*, A Book of Diaries (London: Lindsay Drummond, 1947) p. 42.
9. George Orwell, *The Collected Essays, Journalism, and Letters: Volume II, 1940–43* (New York: Harvest Books, 1968) p. 54.
10. Samuel Hynes, *The Auden Generation* (London: Bodley Head, 1976) p. 81.
11. Personal interview with Roy Fuller, 22 November 1979.
12. I do not mean to imply that all 'journeys' in the poetry of Auden and his followers were 'successful' ones.
13. It is important to remember the awakening interest in Jungian psychology during this period. See, for instance, Maud Bodkin's *Archetypal Patterns in Poetry* (London: Oxford University Press, 1934; 2nd edn 1948) where she recalls the drowned sailor and Jung's emphasis on a regressive voyage into the deep as preliminary to renewal of life.
14. Geoffrey Grigson (ed.), *Poetry of the Present, An Anthology of the Thirties and After* (London: Phoenix House, 1949) p. 13.
15. John Lehmann, *I Am My Brother* (New York: Reynal and Co., 1960) p. 109.
16. Alun Lewis, in Ian Hamilton (ed.), *Selected Poetry and Prose* (London: George Allen & Unwin, 1966). Also see, in addition to 'On Embarkation', 'Song' and 'Water Music', other journey poems: 'A Troopship in the Tropics', 'Port of Call: Brazil', and 'The Journey'.

17. Geoffrey Grigson, 'Twenty-Seven Sonnets', *New Verse* New Series I, no. 2 (May 1939) p. 49.
18. Personal interview with Julian Symons, 7 November 1979.
19. Julian Symons, *Notes from Another Country* (London: London Magazine Editions, 1972) p. 66.
20. Letter from Julian Symons to the author, 12 December 1979.
21. Angus Calder, *The People's War* (New York: Random House, 1979) p. 512.
22. Stephen Spender, *Poetry Since 1939* (London: Longman for the British Council, 1946) p. 112.
23. Ian Hamilton, *The Little Magazines* (London: Weidenfeld & Nicolson, 1976) p. 9.
24. Cyril Connolly, *The Listener*, 5 December 1940, p. 812.
25. Derek Stanford, *Inside the Forties* (London: Sidgwick & Jackson, 1977) p. 91.
26. John Lehmann, *Thrown to the Woolfs* (London: Weidenfeld & Nicolson, 1978) p. 88.
27. Ibid., pp. 88–9.
28. Lehmann, *I Am My Brother*, p. 163.
29. Virginia Woolf, *Between the Acts* (New York: Harcourt Brace Jovanovich, 1969) p. 98.
30. Woolf, *A Writer's Diary*, p. 306.

2 The Apocalyptics and Dylan Thomas

Looking ahead to the 1940s in her last novel, Virginia Woolf feared that the new decade would stifle imaginative activity with a chaos worse than any she had ever known. Looking back from the vantage point of the 1950s, however, the poets and critics of the Movement saw only an imagination gone wild. Woolf's genuine uncertainty about the immediate future led her to pose searching questions in *Between the Acts*; yet retrospection only seemed to endow the fifties commentators with security. The labels and paradigms they applied to the decade behind them were convenient but incorrect. Their characterization of their precursors was, above all, an act of dissociation.[1] Desiring to 'restore' a native poetry marked by restraint, logical argument and a realistic adherence to common life, the poets of the fifties insisted that the forties was a decade of punch-drunk apocalyptic writers, a time of irrational excess, a poetry solely of myth and dream. They dismissed the period as drowning in the illogical unconscious storms of such poets as Henry Treece, J. F. Hendry, and Dylan Thomas.

By emphasizing the subjectivity of the forties, the members of the Movement correctly identified the decade's major artistic shift. For in reacting against what they saw as Auden's main concerns, the writers of the forties had indeed turned towards a more personal and less social poetry. Still, by associating this new subjectivity exclusively with the group known as the Apocalyptics (headed by Hendry and Treece) and by choosing Dylan Thomas as the chief exponent of such excessive tendencies, the Movement critics falsified the period on several major counts.

It is easy to see why the Movement chose the Apocalyptics to typify the activities of the decade preceding them. As the most recent and best-organized group of poets the forties had to offer, the romantic New Apocalypse offered a recognizable target. Yet by making the group stand for the decade, the Movement poets and later critics blurred important distinctions. They failed to separate the Apocalyptics from forerunners such as the Surrealists or from their later incarnations as Personalists or Neo-Romantics. The Movement poets and propagandists ignored the central fact that the Apocalyptics originated in 1938 and probably rose to the peak of their influence in 1941 with their second group anthology rather than exercising an important influence throughout the 1940s. The fifties critics also took no interest in disentangling or relating the secular and religious strands that weave in and out of the poetry of the forties; they glossed over Dylan Thomas' strong detachment from Apocalyptic beliefs and his own development towards a simpler and less private style. And, most ruinous to a characterization of the period, they had little or nothing to say about the best poetry of the war and post-war years. Poets whose reliance on form and tradition is most notable – figures such as Alun Lewis, Sidney Keyes, Keith Douglas, Henry Reed, Bernard Spencer and Roy Fuller – hardly fit the stereotype of 'hysterical' irrationalists which the Movement critics invoked as a foil for their devotion to order and reason.

The literary historian concerned with an accurate assessment of the 1940s must construct a subway map of the period, showing origins, intersections and overlappings of groups and individuals, destinations, and arrival spots. Thus, the Apocalyptics and their forerunners the Surrealists overlapped in their parallel reactions against the Auden school, but the Apocalyptics also dissociated themselves from the Surrealists. Similarly, the kinship between the Apocalyptics and individual poets such as D. H. Lawrence and Gerard Manley Hopkins shows the far-reaching roots of a seemingly freak and spontaneous movement. The contemporary context is also important: the religious revival at the turn of the decade often intersected with the New Apocalypse, though it lacked the group's personal self-absorption. Finally, with more care than the fifties poets and critics could afford, given their polemical purpose, it is important to note the amorphous nature of the Apocalyptics. The best poets who started out as Apocalyptics usually broke away from the group early. G. S. Fraser and Nicholas Moore, for instance, moved towards a simpler and less obscure style.

Because of Dylan Thomas' early relationship to the Apocalyptics, it is instructive to see that even he departs from an early reliance on the obscurities and verbal excesses of Surrealists and Apocalyptics alike. He thus provides the perfect transition from the establishment of the group in 1938 to the younger writers of the 1940s who, like Keith Douglas, were forced by the course of history to practise a less clotted, realistic poetry from the first. That 'other' poetry of the forties – in its simultaneous attention to subjectivity and objectivity, to metaphysics and concrete state-ment – exceeds by far the simplistic labels needed by the fifties poets and by supporters of anti-romantic poetry to promote themselves. It holds in balance the passionate and ironic, the irrational and rational.

I SURREALISM AND ORIGINS OF THE APOCALYPTICS

In addition to criticisms noted earlier, a deliberate romantic rebellion against the Auden generation occurred in the late 1930s and early 1940s. When they banded together (as part of this reaction), the members of the New Apocalypse held very different assumptions about the nature of poetry from other poets of the thirties. Politics was outside the realm of poetry; the private individual imagination was more important than any collective myth kit; and the poet was an inspired bard or visionary. Advertising such beliefs, the Apocalyptics advanced an already widespread tendency to play down man's relationship to society. As Robert Hewison has noted,[2] the Apocalyptics were the 'extremists' in a wave of romanticism that surged through English culture during the war years and affected all the arts. Yet though theoretically opposed to the Auden generation and to all the tenets of a publication such as Geoffrey Grigson's *New Verse*, they found their roots in the same decade. They are, one might say, the products of certain co-ordinating romantic and subjective impulses which could no longer be suppressed in the rationally-controlled yet increasingly apocalyptic climate of the 1930s.

The socially melioristic philosophy of the New Apocalypse grew out of 1930s doctrines. Freud, Marx, and French Surreal-ism, all popular in the 1930s, provided the group with its eclectic basis. The Apocalyptics saw themselves as moralists eager both to free the individual from the constraining systems of a mechanistic universe and to exalt him into the 'godhead' of his own imagination.

The threat of the Second World War, while spurring few poets into the hysterics derided by the Movement critics, did confirm the chaos anticipated by an earlier generation.[3] Stephen Spender wrote of a surrealistic disorder having become a way of life during the war years:

> The immense resources of all the governments of the world are now being devoted to producing surrealistic effects. Surrealism has ceased to be fantasy, its objects hurtle around our heads, its operations cause the strangest conjunctions of phenomena in the most unexpected places, its pronouncements fill the newspapers.[4]

In their drive to exalt man's imagination, the Apocalyptics were thus only codifying ideas prevalent earlier. By the time of the first official anthology, *The New Apocalypse* (1939), many ancestors and influences had made their mark on the group. Surrealism was the most general and important of influences. First popular on the continent in response to the First World War, Surrealism became more popular in England in the 1930s, when translations from the French, original English works and critical studies helped to create an audience fascinated by its 'experiments in automatic writing, its contempt for obvious logic and traditional form, and its use of violently incongruous, apparently meaningless juxtapositions of phrases'.[5] As explained by Henry Treece in his critical work *Dylan Thomas* (finally published in 1949), Surrealism intended to 'shock the world into reconsidering its conception of reality'.[6]

David Gascoyne re-introduced the Surrealists to Britain with his translations and, in 1935, with his historical account, *A Short Survey of Surrealism*, a critical study also featuring translations and illustrations of surrealistic art. In 1936 Gascoyne published *Man's Life is this Meat*, a collection of poems recalling Freudian dreams or symbolist visions of hell: 'An arrow with lips of cheese was caught by a floating hair'. In 1936 he also translated Bréton's *What is Surrealism?* In the same year, Éluard's poems were translated and published in *Thorns of Thunder* edited by George Reavy; Herbert Read published *An Introduction to Surrealism*; the first International Surrealist Exhibition opened in London; and the first issue of Roger Roughton's *Contemporary Poetry and Prose* appeared. For two years Roughton published early poems by Gascoyne and

Thomas. In spite of such a strong impact in the mid-thirties, Surrealism never caught on in England as it had in France. John Heath-Stubbs thinks that England did not respond strongly to Surrealism in literature because she had no need to augment her own native element of the fantastic.[7] She had her own 'Kubla Khan' and rich stores of dream poetry to draw upon.

Most English surrealist poems seem pointless and tedious with their bizarre word associations and shocking juxtapositions. They may well be full of profound implications – a claim made for Gascoyne in his *Collected Poems*[8] – but they actually say very little. A few lines of Gascoyne's, at random, show the worst of what seems to be only an hallucinatory and obsessive game with words and images:

The Cubical Domes

Indeed indeed it is growing very sultry
The Indian feather pots are scrambling out of the room
The slow voice of the tobacconist is like a circle
Drawn on the floor in chalk and containing ants
And indeed there is a show upon the table
And indeed it is as regular as clockwork
Demonstrating the variability of the weather
Or denying the existence of man altogether
For after all why should love resemble a cushion. . . .

Why indeed? With such incoherent products, Surrealism remains more valuable for its aims than for its achievement. Its disgust with society's political mistakes and its own 'political' hopes must be kept in mind. This attitude was rightly stressed by Herbert Read in his essay 'Surrealism and the Romantic Principle', published in 1936 in his *Introduction to Surrealism*. 'Art, we conclude, is more than description or "reportage"; it is a dialectical activity, an act of renewal. It renews vision, it renews language; but more essentially, it renews life itself by enlarging the sensibility, by making man more conscious of the terror and beauty, the wonder of the possible forms of being.'[9] Surrealism was, in its way, as moralistic as Auden's poetry, though it continued to be regarded in England as a reaction against Auden. Its advocacy of semi-automatic writing and an associative process of creation seemed to support an increasing distrust in the failures

of the rational, socio-political mind, now blamed for such
'accomplishments' as the Depression and the Spanish Civil War.

Already a major advocate of the Surrealists, Herbert Read also
emerged as a spokesman of the Apocalyptics in articles such as
'The New Romantic School' (*The Listener*, 1942) where he
heralded a sweeping romanticism: 'Now we might say, of the
whole youthful movement that has gathered in these last few years
that it is an English version of Surrealism'.[10] Read refers to the
New Apocalypse as 'Surrealism with a difference' without really
explaining what that difference is. But an early theoretician for
the Apocalyptics, G. S. Fraser, defined it in the second group
anthology, *The White Horseman* (1941):

> Apocalypse in a sense derives from Surrealism, and one might
> even call it a dialectical development of it; the next stage
> forward. It embodies what is positive in Surrealism. It denies
> what is negative – Surrealism's own denial of man's right to
> exercise conscious control, either of his own political and social
> destinies or of the material offered to him, as an artist, by his
> subconscious mind. It recognizes that is, that the intellect and
> its activity in willed action is part of the living completeness of
> art.[11]

Fraser has amplified this preface in personal conversation.[12] He
felt, he told me, that the Surrealist school in France (like the
Symbolists before them) had developed a philosophical attitude
towards poetry. A poem didn't necessarily mean something, it
just existed, and one need not explain or elucidate it. 'Bréton
seemed to be saying that you could ignore the social structuring of
language and audience. You could express emotion directly.' It
was this element of Surrealism that especially appealed to the
Apocalyptics. Still, whereas the Surrealists refused to exercise
control over any material thrown up by the unconscious self, the
writers of the New Apocalypse also rejected an enslavement by
the subconscious workings of the mind. J. F. Hendry wrote:
'Artists more responsible than Surrealists find that art is not
merely the juxtaposition of images not commonly juxtaposed, but
the recognition, the communication of organic experience,
experience with a personal shape, experience which (however
wild and startling in content) is a formal whole'.[13] The Apocalyptics thus preferred to impose form on subconscious material, to

give it a distinct shape. As G. S. Fraser later explained, the Apocalyptics submitted to an inner logic, a 'dream logic in images' which originated in the subconscious mind.

The destruction of a social world was forcing the poet back on himself for a sense of identity and purpose. While the Surrealists mocked a collapsing society in the 1930s, the Apocalyptics faced even greater chaos. Absurdist tactics were no longer useful; now the writer tried to reconstruct something out of his own inner chaos. Henry Treece, who had viewed Surrealism as 'a movement with a mission',[14] viewed the New Apocalypse in the same terms, but the mission and intentions had changed.

In the summer of 1938 the magazine *Seven* began publication; opposing the influence of *New Verse* and *New Writing*, it also prepared the way for the New Apocalypse. Nicholas Moore, the managing editor, was soon to be a contributor to the Apocalyptic anthology. But it was the financier and publisher of *Seven*, John Goodland, one of history's forgotten, who launched the idea of the New Apocalypse. On 15 October he wrote to Henry Treece from King's College, Cambridge, to suggest an anthology of prose and verse: 'I suppose this thing will fulfil two functions, to debunk Auden and the whole *New Signatures-Verse-Writing* generation, and also to put forward another idea – that of apocalyptic writings.'[15] This movement was soon under way. After corresponding and meeting with each other, the literary spokesmen Hendry and Treece produced a manifesto. Paraphrased by Francis Scarfe in his book *Auden and After*, the credo postulated four central points:[16]

1. Man was in need of a greater freedom, economic no less than aesthetic, from machines and mechanistic thinking.
2. No existent political system, Left or Right; no artistic ideology, Surrealism or a political school like Auden's could lead to this freedom.
3. The machine age exerted too strong an influence on art and prevented individual development of man.
4. Myth, as a personal means of reintegrating the personality, had been neglected and despised.

Three anthologies sprung from these assertions: *The New Apocalypse* (1939), *The White Horseman* (1941) and *The Crown and the Sickle* (1945). The original contributors in 1938 included Henry Treece, J. F. Hendry, Norman MacCaig, Nicholas Moore, Philip O'Connor, Robert Melville, and Dylan Thomas.

I INFLUENCES AND ANALOGUES

Stalwartly defending man's individuality in the face of great dehumanizing forces, the Apocalyptics also appropriated certain romantic tendencies found in earlier writers. Their concern with the violence of modern life, their plumbing the subconscious depths, their explorations with language, their interest in private vision, their use of myth and dream, and their startling and original diction find associates and progenitors in D. H. Lawrence, Robert Graves, George Barker and Gerard Manley Hopkins. Dylan Thomas was also a major stylistic influence, though at no time a pledged member of the Apocalyptics.

Against poets who were 'sacrificing the individual',[17] Treece called for a figurehead of the movement who promoted the 'I': D. H. Lawrence.[18] An unpublished letter from J. F. Hendry to Henry Treece reveals the importance of Lawrence's book *Apocalypse* and its symbology to the group. On 5 October 1940, Hendry urged Treece: 'Read if you haven't done so Lawrence's *Apocolypse* ... We must have a quote from him'.[19] In the posthumous 1932 work, Lawrence had cast the First Horseman of the Apocalypse as a symbol for man's inner self. And the group used the following quotation as the epigraph to their second anthology, *The White Horseman*:

> The rider on the white horse! Who is he then? . . . He is the royal me, he is my very self and his horse is the whole MANA of a man. He is my very me, my sacred ego, called into a new cycle of action by the Lamb and riding forth to conquest, the conquest of the old self for the birth of a new self.

Besides providing them with a central symbol and tag words such as *organicism*, Lawrence also offered a theory of poetic creation based on images that sounded remarkably like that of Dylan Thomas. He further affected the Apocalyptics by buttressing their interest in the psychology of the unconscious.

But the first British poet to make a full intellectual use of unconscious states of mind was Robert Graves. The destructive power of the earlier world war emerged most dramatically in poems he wrote between 1920 and 1923. These poems activate the horrors of recent war experiences and resort to creativity as a form of therapy. A sanity, quite absent in surrealistic works, informs them – for while Graves writes mimetically of horror, he never abdicates a firm control. As Geoffrey Bullough shrewdly suggests: his poetry becomes 'cerebral and metaphysical not so much by its abstraction and wit, but by its pre-occupation with psychological problems, the relativity of knowledge, the problems of identity, discontinuity of experience, dissociation of personality'.[20] Such extreme poems as 'The Pier Glass', which documents anguish, or 'Down' (a half-riddle, half-nightmare) illustrate the mental storms which helped further a poetry of the unconscious.

George Barker was closest to Thomas in stylistic influence on the Apocalyptics. He had never succumbed to the allurements of Surrealism though he achieved similar effects. His most famous poem 'Calamiterror' (1937), a long 'symphonic' poem as Scarfe dubbed it,[21] recalled the violently juxtaposed images of Eliot's *The Waste Land*. In fact, it is this very emphasis on image and the forcefulness of his juxtapositions that made Barker an influence on the New Apocalypse though he did not take the extra step of fusing disparate images, as Thomas did. In his important article 'The Miracle of Images', published by John Lehmann in *Orpheus* 2, 1949, Barker summed up his desire to startle the reader without a surrealistic association of images. Referring to stock images found together in Surrealistic poems, Barker contended: 'The Surrealists were myopic. They failed to observe that what was remarkable was neither the sewing machine, nor the umbrella nor the dissecting table nor the effect produced by this encounter, but the space in between'.[22] Barker's poems presented records of a chaotic disintegrating world.

Other poets and critics indirectly helped in crystallizing the neo-romantic revival of the Apocalyptics. Gerard Manley Hopkins may seem an odd influence for the 1940s, considering that the Laureate Robert Bridges had edited his poems as far back as 1918. But it was actually through Charles Williams' 1930 edition that Hopkins became more widely appreciated. In his introduction, Williams, who in the next decade would be part of his own intellectual group stressing myth, dream and realms beyond pure logic,[23] praised Hopkins for his 'Passionate emotion; his passionate intellect which is striving at once to recognize and explain both the singleness and division of the accepted Universe', and his 'passionate consciousness of all kinds of experience'.[24] Henry Treece was drawn to this introduction and to similarities between the verbal inventions of Hopkins and of Dylan Thomas while writing his critical work on Thomas. He was prompted to compose a chapter on 'The Debt to Hopkins' (though published in 1949, the critical study was being researched in the early 1940s). Treece's chapter, which startled even Thomas because of the stylistic similarities set forth,[25] noted of Hopkins that 'his manner rather than his matter influences'. At the head of the chapter, Treece quoted the Williams laudation, obviously drawn to a violent, energetic Hopkins-in-Thomas. Fascinated by the rhythmic linguistic pirouettes of Hopkins, Treece called attention to the flexible mind responsible for them. He saw a similar flexibility in Thomas and recommended the Welshman as a model to his colleagues: Thomas is, following Hopkins, he says, 'a poet of conflict, of intensity and rebellion in a way, and to a degree unapproached by any other poet of his period'.[26] Clearly favouring revolt in art and life, Treece claims that the work of a poet like Hopkins is remarkable for its 'tension, a dissatisfaction with accepted formulae, yet a hope for the future'. Such thoughts found their way directly into various essays written by Fraser, Treece and Hendry in the New Apocalypse anthologies.

If the Apocalyptics were drawn to Hopkins for his energetic use of language and his somersaulting style, other intellectuals were consoled by his 'classical' Christology. For in the late 1930s and early 1940s a philosophical and religious revival made its way directly into poetry. What unites all the influences, predecessors, and analogues: Surrealists, Lawrence, Graves, Barker, Hopkins, Thomas, is an interest in parts of the imagination not controlled by reason and logic. Their interests in the passions and the subconscious paralleled a new reliance in others on faith and belief.

Some poets, like the young Derek Stanford, turned to a philosophy of Introversion. Kierkegaard, he has written in his memoirs, 'was enriching both my reflective and meditative powers' though 'I was not replacing a political with a religious world picture'.[27] Other poets, however, were moving towards a more strongly religious centre. Book reviews and editorials in the *TLS* at the turn of the decade are testaments to this growing spiritual revival. For instance, an article called 'The Invincible Reality' (23 September 1939) recommends Jacques Maritain's *True Humanism* for a philosophy transcending 'the destructive individualism which has brought the modern world to its present pass'. Other influential books of the time included George Every's

Christian Discrimination (1940) and W. Osborne Greenwood's *Christianity and the Mechanists* (1941) which stresses (from the scientific viewpoint) that due to the successful mechanical method in biology and physics, the last generation dismissed theological and philosophical views too hastily. The major poem of the 1940s, of course, was Eliot's *Four Quartets*. *Burnt Norton* was originally published in Eliot's *Collected Poems 1909–1935*. After the success of *East Coker* in 1940, it was reprinted as a pamphlet and the four were published together in 1944. This masterpiece which grew directly from personal experience is, above all, a meditation on time and eternity. In literary histories it seems to stand alone. Yet it finds its larger context in the philosophical and religious revival. A poet of the older generation, Edith Sitwell, also wrote moving, and popular, religious poetry in the early 1940s. *Street Songs* (1942) is perhaps best known for its lyric 'Still Falls the Rain'. Besides Sitwell, other poets turned to sacred imagery and themes, poets such as Anne Ridler who was helped early in her career by the older Eliot. David Gascoyne, Vernon Watkins, Kathleen Raine and Dylan Thomas meet on common ground with Hendry and others in their use of Christian symbolism. Even Treece himself felt in his own work a 'growing simplicity and religious observance'.[28]

In his collection of essays *The Thirties and After*, Stephen Spender has remarked on this resurgence of the spiritual. He credits it to be the 'seriousness of the constant confrontation with death and destruction',[29] certainly part of the cause. In 1943, Norman Nicholson, one of the major spokesmen for the shift in values, summed it up differently: 'I believe there is a new humility, and a new realisation that man is an imperfect, sinful, dependent being; that planning and politics, however necessary and important, are not in themselves enough'.[30] The year before, Nicholson had published one of the major forties documents for a Christian point of view, *An Anthology of Religious Verse* including works such as Gascoyne's 'Pietà', Eliot's 'We Praise Thee' from *Murder in the Cathedral*, and the Ship of Death sequence from Lawrence's *Last Poems*. Nicholson grouped the poems under such headings as 'Worship' and 'Gloria'. 'To many modern poets', asserted Nicholson, 'the events of our Lord's life are so vivid that they seem to be contemporary, so that it is natural for them to write it in the language, imagery and form of our time'.[31]

The private world of intuition and metaphysics was more

important to poets of the 1940s than the political and intellectual world of the 1930s. And it is easy to stereotype the period as romantic and irrational; yet part of that irrationality was absorbed into systems of belief. Further, even the most 'irrational' of poets, such as Gascoyne and Thomas, changed direction as the war continued. Robert Hewison has called attention to a shift in Gascoyne's poetry[32] – that shift, which aims to engage the purely magical in a structured combat with realism, had already occurred in the poetry of others. Gascoyne wrote in an introduction to his section of the Hogarth Press anthology *Poets of Tomorrow, Third Selection* (1942): 'In the long run it [poetry of the "magical quality"] is probably less rewarding, less consoling, than that resulting from conflict between the instinctive poetic impulse and the impersonal discipline, the unadorned sobriety of realistic "sense".' Structured by faith and meditation, or at war with a more realistic poetry, the purely magical and irrational did not exercise a lasting or wide influence.

III THE APOCALYPTICS AND LATER INCARNATIONS

At first when the Apocalyptics found a reading public, they were lauded for turning away from 'reportage' to dream life. *The White Horseman*, reviewed in *TLS* (6 September 1941), was noted as part of a new trend of 'integrity' in poetry.

> The interest of the movement for which Mr. Fraser speaks and the group who contribute to this anthology is that they are seeking beneath the social and political surface, with which their predecessors were often arbitrarily concerned, for the perennial roots of poetry in the imagination itself, believing that in 'stripping the individual darkness from their own wills' they will 'not only become truer poets but bring that integrated society which a poet needs'.[33]

In the *TLS* of 16 May 1942, Treece was still earning praise. Discussing *Invitation and Warning*, the reviewer comments: 'He plucks a new and often baffling music out of a familiar instrument. His imagination creates a true mythology – in his power to do this he is essentially a poet and his craft is as individual as his dreaming'.[34] Critics began to look to the Apocalyptics as leaders in a restoration of the full-blooded imagination and as rebels leaving the reign of Auden.

However, critics even then were not wholly laudatory about the new poetic school. Of all styles, the Apocalyptic gave way to what Fraser has since called 'various kinds of faking'.[35] Often the images chosen were unclear and unorganized. Thus the Apocalyptics encouraged, though not meaning to do so, a laxity in their less gifted writers or, worse still, imitative writing among their best. Shocking the reader into a new awareness often meant poetic haemorrhage, as in Hendry's poem 'Golgotha' from *The White Horseman*, itself reminiscent of Thomas' 'Altarwise by Owl-Light'.

Golgotha

Crow, wooden lightning, from a sky of thorn –
O cross-ribbed Adam, tumbled hill of blood,
While blinded shell and body's thunder churn
Ear to worm-ball, tongue to lipless stone.

At their weakest, these poets shared a heavy reliance on purely literary images and diction and a common inability to provide one controlling idea per poem. Peter Wells' 'Poem in Time of Famine' from *The Crown and the Sickle* provides such a welter of images:

You now with a green nettle nestling in your hair,
Wandering with shallow, hollow feet over stones I cannot
    comb:
In your eye light like steeples striking gaunt with the hunger
    of your bell's chiming:
And the wolf roars famine where the war's axle twists in the
    mire
And the spas of oil heap on your starred, seven-compassed
    eye.

Reviewing Treece's volume *Invitation and Warning* for *Scrutiny* in Summer 1942, D. J. Enright mocked the easy writing of such 'semi-surrealists': 'When he can't go on non-meaning any longer he can always indulge in a little meaning'. According to Enright, whose review is negative in the balance, Treece is representative of a surrealist type of 'Bogeyland'. 'His poems are thus compiled from a prescribed set of images – iron, knife, blood, bones, heart, ghosts, miscellaneous Hamletry, God (or god), the fairy tale paraphernalia of prince, goose girl, pear-tree, and roses, and so on: "My tale of horror was the dry-dugged virgin, / The eyeless child with flowers in his claw." ' [36]

Other critics, such as John Singer in a *Poetry Quarterly* review of *The Crown and the Sickle*, point to the mass of contradictions within the group and question the very existence of an Apocalyptic style. He too complains of pastiche, of heart-throbbing verses without a proper muse. 'Real schools', he argues, 'like real historical movements, grow defined and appraisable only after certain determined periods. Contemporary witnesses are guessing. My guess is that the emotive cohesion and eventual motive behind the label "Apocalyptic Writing" is too amorphous and immediately pointless for collective assessment. The label remains merely a cryptic slogan, its very employment the "object" Hendry warns us against'.[37]

In all the poetry of the Apocalyptics, the subjective vision seems to screen reality behind a tapestry of crosses, thorns, princes, rock, and light shot with crimson. The Apocalyptics confront war but not in terms of particularized events or in specifically human occasions. Instead of dealing directly with war's realities, they romanticize destruction.

Perhaps inevitably, the 'school' spread thin and dissolved. It was vague from the start. Even more important, the individual talents of its members required other avenues of expression. G. S. Fraser, for instance, found his own voice (more Apollonian than Dionysian) during his war service in Cairo and after. His association with the group had been tenuous. Though he wrote one of their major manifestoes – the introduction to the second anthology, *The White Horseman* – his reasons for doing so were mixed. He sympathized with their enmity towards 'a false objectivism, a tendency to create pseudo-scientific systems of politics, ethics, theology . . . as the most dangerous tendency' of the times.[38] In a review of *The New Apocalypse*, from which the previous remarks come, he compares this first anthology to *Lyrical Ballads*. Wordsworth's collection contains some bad verse, he proclaims, but is important because it 'takes a stand'. A willing ally, he was publicly advanced to the ranks of leader partly because he courted the opportunity offered for publishing. Under the Apocalyptic label, Fraser was published by Routledge. In the years to follow he established himself as an important, if minor, English poet.

A comparison of certain lines from his poems of the 1940s shows the emergence of his more realistic and disciplined style:

From 'City of Benares', 1941:

Deeper than grief can plummet, mercy lies
But not so deep as trust in children's eyes,
Justice is high in heaven, but more high
Blood of the innocent shall smear the sky –
Or think that red the flame of seraph wings,
See stained-glass heaven, where each darling sings
In God's dark luminous world of green and gold

From 'Two Short Poems', 1941:

Ah, my sister, let's not dream
Like a boy who butts the wind,
Time will e'er be less unkind.
Gaze not in the crystal stream,
Lilies none, or leaves, it yields.
Winter savages the fields.

From 'The Traveller has Regrets', 1948:

The traveller has regrets
For the receding shore
That with its many nets
Has caught, not to restore,
The white lights in the bay,
The blue lights on the hill,
Though night with many stars
May travel with him still.

In a 1953 collection of some of his poems, published in Japan, G. S. Fraser commented on his own poetry and influences; he did not include the Apocalyptics. He felt himself representative because of theme: the anxiety of our time, the impact of foreign places, of exile and loneliness, of strong feelings about distant home and family. He credited certain poets with a permanent place in his poetic memory: Yeats, Pound, Auden and (for conversational diction), Pope, Byron, Clough, Browning. Yet he called his volume *Leaves Without a Tree* because he felt part of no central tradition within English poetry itself.[39] In 'The Human Situation' Fraser sounds as un-apocalyptic as possible:

> We cannot promise but can pray,
> For help upon the human way
> From hate and error quiet release.

Nicholas Moore, though less interesting than Fraser, provides another example of a sympathetic contributor who moved away from the group's rich diction and mythic imagery. 'The Flag', one of several poems contributed to the 1941 anthology opens:

> O my star shine, O my sun weep,
> The red peeps over the pillow into my river.
> O God I bleed for all the bloody world,
> The torture that I cannot keep.

His later poems attain a greater simplicity in spite of consistently romantic diction:

> That the air was cold and grey, the skies blue
> With hover of clouds, white clouds, and the wind shrill
> Was all that they, in their earnest converse, could tell.
>
> ('A Scene in November')

As the war continued, the New Apocalypse lost some early members. Dispersing, yet also gaining new voices such as Robert Herring, Alex Comfort and Wrey Gardiner, the group became known as Neo-Romanticism. Throughout the 1940s, neo-romantic anthologies and magazines were published regularly. Alex Comfort and Robert Graecen edited *Lyra* with an introduction by Herbert Read. Comfort joined John Bayliss in editing the first two numbers of *New Road* in 1943 and 1944. 'It all makes generous reading', declared one reviewer (*TLS*, 2 September 1944) yet adds the honest reservation, 'very naturally a camp follower is likely to get most pleasure or excitement from the reading'.

Though from the mid-1940s the poets of the New Apocalypse and Neo-Romanticism were popular more as individuals than as a group, the desire for a group was kept alive. Treece already spoke of his Apocalyptics disbanding in *Transformation* (1943), an anthology edited with Stefan Schimanski. Yet there he and Schimanski also proposed a new group, Personalism. Sounding remarkably like the New Apocalypse, Personalism, they explained, was different. 'Its survey of personality is wider-reaching, broader rather than deeper.'[40] Forced to abandon the idea of a unified group, Treece and Schimanski still continued their ceaseless efforts towards defining and promoting a purely romantic poetry. In 1949 they persisted: 'If Classicism is sunlight Romanticism is black midnight and the Northern Lights hanging their coloured curtains in the sky. If Classicism is science, knowledge, defined and definite, Romanticism is that fantasy and speculation which allows man a brief glimpse of his godhead'.[41] They persisted, but the 'mission' to fight a war of Romantic against Classic had become outworn and tired. When the battle occurred, it took place within single poems or single poets. And often there was not conflict, but truce.

IV   DYLAN THOMAS, THE EARLY POETRY

Just as it is simplistic to stereotype the 1940s as a decade of irrational excess so Movement poets and later critics incorrectly labelled Dylan Thomas. Propagandists for the Movement cast him as both a Surrealist and as an Apocalyptic, but because of his own individuality, he fits neither slot. He does write 'inward' poetry, which is characteristic of the 1940s, but actually his poetry of the 1930s is more incoherent in comparison with what follows. Early volumes: *18 Poems* (1934), *25 Poems* (1936), and *A Map of Love* (1939), reflect a groping towards less self-orientation and a greater directness. He became more aware of audience as he progressed. Dissociating himself from surrealistic and apocalyptic styles, he achieved a more communicative poetry.

Thomas was branded early for writing confused and confusing (though somehow haunting) poems. Torrid lines such as these at first seem impenetrable:

> I, in my intricate image, stride on two levels,
> Forged in man's minerals, the brassy orator
> Laying my ghost in metal,
> The scales of this twin world tread on the double,
> My half ghost in armour hold hard in death's corridor,
> To my man-iron sidle.
>
> ('I, in My Intricate Image')

or

> How soon the servant sun,
> (Sir morrow mark),
> Can time unriddle, and the cupboard stone,
> (Fog has a bone
> He'll trumpet into meat)
>
> ('How Soon the Servant Sun')

In passages such as these, single images puff up with the riddling quality of Gascoyne's: *man-iron sidle* and *trumpet into meat* or *star-flanked seed* and *four-stringed hill*. Inventing words like *sea-spindle* and *pin-hilled*. Thomas played with words and recorded half-processed ideas and feelings. In a 1935 letter to his editor Richard Church,[42] he denied the taint of Surrealism, but he knew Gascoyne and Roughton, and must have read poems printed alongside his own in *New Verse* and *Contemporary Poetry and Prose*.

Thomas opened a larger world for the Apocalyptics. For them he acted as a mediator between the chaotic verses of the school of Bréton and Éluard and the too-controlled practices of the Auden school. In their desire to escape rational controls, the Apocalyptics warmed to Thomas' romantic theory of composition. Basing his theory on the image, he suggested a method of composition with obvious connections to Freudian dream psychology:

I make one image – though 'make' is not the word; I let, perhaps an image to be 'made' emotionally in me and then apply to it what intellectual and critical forces I possess – let it breed another, let that image contradict the first, make of the third image bred out of the other two together; a fourth contradictory image, and let them all, within my imposed formal limits, conflict. Each image holds within it the seed of its own destruction, and my dialectical method, as I understand it, is a constant building up and breaking down of the images that came out of the central seed, which is itself destructive and constructive at the same time.[43]

Paul C. Ray has cogently described the process in his book *The Surrealist Movement in England*. The method, he says, goes one step beyond the comparative function of simile or metaphor; it is the *fusion* of two elements which are unlike. If image A evokes image B, and image C evokes image D, B can be fused with D. Thus if image A is sexuality and evokes B which is hair; and if image C, Eden, evokes D which is apple, we may get the phrase and image: *bearded apple* (from 'Incarnate Devil').[44] This tortured process of associating each image shows us that Thomas' seemingly unrelated images are connected to each other, if only by a private inner logic. In her study of Thomas' poetry worksheets, Lita Hornick has also stressed that he worked from rational principles towards hallucinatory effects of the irrational.[45] In fact, Thomas was exacting in his attempt to create what he termed a formally 'watertight compartment of words'. (*New Verse*, 11 October 1934.)

The Apocalyptics determined that Thomas walked a saner path than the Surrealists. They were attracted to his fusion of the rational and irrational, the conscious and the subconscious. They also responded strongly to his subject matter – biological rather than historical, anarchic in a non-political way, almost primitive in its intensity. Finally, the Freudian aspect of his poetry, especially the overt sexual meanings he explored with themes of love, life-cycles and religion, appealed to their own credo of Man over the Machine. Treece's testimony to Dylan Thomas was considered a manual for the other Apocalyptics: 'A terror of the darkness, a fear of hidden things . . . In bringing them to light the poet teaches himself and some of us, to grapple with them and overcome them'.[46]

The special charisma Thomas exercised over some of these English writers owed much to his staunch individuality. Even in his refusal to sign the Apocalyptic Manifesto, he emerged a leader. Scornful of poets he regarded as lesser talents, Thomas vowed to have nothing to do with the group. Only financial reasons led him to publish in *The New Apocalypse*. In an unpublished letter to John Goodland, Thomas intimated that he had received a contributors' list and some information about both the anthology and the manifesto. He also questioned the use of the word apocalyptic to describe these writers.[47] Eight days later on 31 December 1938, Thomas refused Treece's request to sign the manifesto and join the group: 'Answering your first letter: I won't sign, with or without argument, the Apocalyptic Manifesto. I wouldn't sign any manifesto unless I had written every word of it, and then I might be too ashamed. I agree with it and like much of it, and some of it, I think, is manifestly absurd.'[48]

Of use to the Apocalyptics but never committed to them, Dylan Thomas was regarded by discriminating critics as a detachable member of their romantic revival. In an early review George Orwell noted how Thomas' immense promise utterly separated him from the other contributors to *The White Horseman*. In *Life and Letters To-Day*, Orwell refers to the Apocalyptics as 'Surrealists with the brake on'. He hints that the poems of the anthology will not be remembered in the next decade but refuses to extend his prediction to Thomas. In fact, Orwell seems slightly surprised that Thomas published with the group. 'The one thing that suggests I may be wrong', he admits concerning the value of the book, 'is that the group includes Dylan Thomas, who in his queer way is certainly something out of the common'. Praising Thomas for extracting 'music from words', Orwell dubs him 'that almost extinct creature, a lyric poet' and claims that such talent is innate and only doubtfully useful for the founding of 'schools'.[49] Fully aware of his promotion of Thomas apart from the others, Orwell confided to Rayner Heppenstall (11 April 1940) that he 'took the opportunity' in this review of 'giving a boost to Dylan, whose stuff I have decided I really like in a way'.[50] Clearly there was some element in Thomas absent from the others which drew even such a socio-political writer as Orwell to praise him.

Unlike Orwell, however, the poets and critics of the 1950s chose to see Thomas as a self-absorbed obscurantist – the archetypal poet of the 1940s. The accusation, once again, tells more about the accusers than their target. Some of Thomas' lines and images are severed from reality and difficult to understand, as we have seen. While Thomas would want us to 'feel' the poetry without necessarily 'understanding' it, he does move towards a more easily comprehended style. Already in the 1930s there are two distinct Dylan Thomases: one appearing Surrealistic or Apocalyptic and the other progressing steadily from obscurities to the simpler and more direct style which would come to fruition in the 1940s. Thomas thus fails to meet the indictment on two counts. He is less obscure during the 1940s, and when he is, he is aware of image-riddles as a defect.

Two stanzas from the 1930s display major changes or oscillations. At times he is so immersed in his own experience that he leaves the reader on the shoals:

> When once the twilight locks no longer
> Locking in the long worm of my finger
> Nor damned the sea that sped about my fist,
> The mouth of time sucked, like a sponge,
> The milky acid on each hinge,
> And swallowed dry the waters of the breast.
>
> ('When Once the Twilight Locks
> No Longer')

Posing similar difficulties are such poems as 'My Hero Bares His Nerves' and 'Altarwise by Owl-Light'.

Around the very same time, however, Thomas managed perfectly understandable verses such as these:

> Light breaks where no sun shines;
> Where no sea runs, the waters of the heart
> Push in their tides;
> And, broken ghosts with glow-worms in their heads,
> The things of light
> File through the flesh where no flesh decks the bones.
>
> ('Light Breaks Where No Sun
> Shines')

'After the Funeral, In Memory of Ann Jones', written in 1933 though published later in 1939, shows the first signs of Thomas' turning outward. He bases the poem on a woman whom he knew, and his response to her death is full and complex; the poem is also clear of fussy confusing images:

> I know her scrubbed and sour humble hands
> Lie with religion in their cramp, her threadbare
> Whisper in a damp word, her wits drilled hollow,
> Her fist of a face died clenched on a round pain;
> And sculptured Ann is seventy years of stone.

While some of his early poetry is overly self-conscious and wildly rhetorical, much of what seems drunkenly abandoned is really very structured. Poems are formed around certain repeated, bardic sentences such as in 'I, in My Intricate Image': 'I, in my intricate image, stride on two levels' (from stanza one); 'I in my fusion of rose and male motion' (from stanza three); 'Beginning with doom in the ghost, and the springing marvels' (from stanza three), and 'Beginning with doom in the bulb, the spring unravels' (from stanza two). Lines tend to be formulaic not only within poems, but from one poem to another, as: 'Where once the waters of your face', 'Where once your green knots sank their splice', 'When once the twilight locks no longer', or 'Shall the star-flanked seed be riddled', 'Shall the hero-in-tomorrow', 'Shall rainbows be their tunics' colour', 'Shall a white answer echo from the rooftops'. Furthermore, the rhymes and half-rhymes are carefully patterned and mutually support the nugget-phrases and lines. Concerned with origins and process as themes, Thomas shapes his work to actively convey the organic energy he celebrates.

If the Movement poets thought that Thomas wrote an asyntactical and disordered poetry, Thomas himself, paradoxically, thought the reverse. He felt in his early verse a lack of spontaneity, a temptation to order and sculpt poetry (even as he memorialized Ann Jones in stone), instead of drawing it out into music. Such disciplined craftsmanship, he felt, could result in obscurity. When Treece suggested to him that his verse was too diffuse, Thomas replied that it might be obscure, but not diffuse: 'My poems *are* formed; they are neither turned on like a tap at all; they are "watertight compartments". Much of the obscurity is due to rigorous compression; the last thing they do is flow; they are much rather hewn'.[51]

V THOMAS IN THE 1940s

While Thomas still refused, as firmly as before, to deal with a political or social reality except in abstract metaphysical terms,[52] his poetry nonetheless seemed to harden further during the war years. In autumn 1940 Thomas moved from Laugharne to London and began a job with Strand Films. During this time he also wrote scripts for the BBC. The war did not find its way into the foreground of Thomas' poems. Shocked and amazed by it, he was especially moved by a film assignment concerning bombing raids. That horror remained engraved in his mind. According to G. S. Fraser and Stephen Spender,[53] war helped Thomas' poetry by giving him a theme without harmfully altering his imagery. Providing background for several of his most magnificent poems, including 'A Refusal to Mourn the Death, By Fire, of a Child in London', war did seem to steady the groundings in reality Thomas had already made.

In 'A Refusal to Mourn', written in 1945, Thomas allows history to enter and inform his private world. He does not refuse to respond to the war death, he only declines to mourn it in the ordinary sense. The interest and special beauty of this poem lie in its treatment of the finality of death in terms of eternity. Sensing that words are inadequate to describe death, Thomas chooses to evoke its blow by sound and suggestion. He breaks sentences sharply, and builds mid-line rhymes and half-lines into a tightly-knit structure. But the active participles *making, fathering, humbling, tumbling, burning, going, unmourning, riding*, forbid this structure from becoming relentlessly confining or cold. The result is a reaction to war and to death different from any other:

> Never until the mankind making
> Bird and beast and flower
> Fathering and all humbling darkness
> Tells with silence the last light breaking
> And the still hour
> Is come of the sea tumbling in harness
>
> And I must enter again the round
> Zion of the water bead
> And the synagogue of the ear of corn
> Shall I let pray the shadow of a sound
> Or sow my salt seed
> In the least valley of sackcloth to mourn
>
> The majesty and burning of the child's death.
> I shall not murder
> The mankind of her going with a grave truth
> Nor blaspheme down the stations of the breath
> With any further
> Elegy of innocence and youth.

Deep with the first dead lies London's daughter,
Robed in the long friends,
The grains beyond age, the dark veins of her mother,
Secret by the unmourning water
Of the riding Thames.
After the first death, there is no other.

In spite of the professed inadequacy of words to capture death, the poem finds a wealth through negation. Thomas does not really refuse to mourn, he just postpones it until all things return to their original darkness. His tone is humbled in the face of darkness and cyclical time.

Stanza two describes the death awaiting all men. When he is dead, the poet's only sound will be prayer, his only mourning will be in the 'least valley of sackcloth'. When he enters the *round* circle of eternity (a darkness here made more sacred by religious imagery), he will not return to a void, but to a sacred and natural place. Having shown death to be positive with two negatives, Thomas introduces the child's death in stanza three.

Filled with anger at those who murder or blaspheme by writing elegies, Thomas vows, 'I shall not murder'. Repeating the idea of his title, he also means that he shall have none of murder, but will give life. He will not provide *grave truth*; he will not write an elegy that is itself a *grave* constructed of words. In the last three lines of the stanza, he appears to derogate Christ by punning on 'stations of the Cross' with 'stations of the breath'. But he actually raises all living things in importance. By their very *breath* they make 'stations of the cross' to an eternal life. There is a mystery and grandeur to all organic life. Thomas fuses the Christian story, the eternal, and the physical, with each element assuming characteristics of the other, just as he did in stanza two. There the Judaic *synagogue* and *Zion* are fused with the physical *water bead* and *ear of corn* (both gifts of a plentiful nature and emblems for male and female sexuality).

The last stanza shows London's daughter stripped of her parental home. Yet she is really not stripped at all. Mother earth and father darkness now nurture her and she is *robed*. Whether physically naked or not, she is increased, not lessened. Lying deep with the first dead, the child becomes as important as all the dead who are fused with the eternal spirit, and with the eternal earth. All are equal in a realm outside time, drenched in silence.

The ceremony of sound in 'A Refusal to Mourn' praises life and eternity – bird, beast and flower, fathering and all humbling darkness, the sea tumbling, the unmourning river of the riding Thames. Death is not to be grieved but remains a secret part of the universal rhythm of remembrance, an entrance, not an exit.

NOTES

1. By implication or explicitly, as individuals and as a group, the Movement criticized its immediate precursors. Howard Sergeant has suggested in 'The Movement – An Agreed Fiction?' in Dannie Abse (ed.), *Best Poetry of the Year 6* (London: Robson Books, 1979), that the propagandists for the Movement made initial attacks on the 1940s, and promoted the idea that a Movement poet was by nature antagonistic to the preceding two decades. In J. D. Scott's announcement of the Movement on the literary stage (*The Spectator*, 1 October 1954), he wrote: the movement is 'bored by the despair of the forties, not much interested in suffering, and extremely impatient of poetic sensibility, especially poetic sensibility about "the writer and society" . . . the Movement, as well as being anti-phoney, is anti-wet; sceptical, robust, ironic, prepared to be as comfortable as possible in a wicked, commercial, threatened world. . . .' According to a myth about the forties, it seemed that the only writers after the Auden generation were Surrealists and the New Apocalypse. The Movement's special mission was to deliver poetry from decadence.

   In the introduction to *New Lines*, a major anthology of Movement poets, Robert Conquest is hazy about whom in the 1940s he is opposing: 'Poets were encouraged to produce diffuse and sentimental verbiage, or hollow technical pirouettes'. He attacks the period, the public taste, and 'poets'. The 'dozen writers' who wrote 'fine verse' through the decade are not named and are conveniently forgotten. In contrast to the 1940s poets, the poets of the 1950s, says Conquest, refuse 'to abandon a rational structure and comprehensible language, even when the verse is most highly charged with emotional intent'. Other important documents include John Wain's promotion of William Empson's 'passion, logic, and formal beauty' in John Lehmann (ed.), *Penguin New Writing*, 40 (1950), p. 127. Empson would become an important influence on the Movement. Also see Wain's early review of Dylan Thomas, published in *Preliminary Essays*, where praise is very strained. See also, Elizabeth Jennings' *An Anthology of Modern Verse 1940–60* and D. J. Enright's *Poets of the 1950s*. Individual poems are also comments on the obscure or over-passionate poetry of the 1940s, such as Donald Davie's 'Poem As Abstract': 'A poem is less an orange than a grid;/It hoists a charge; it does not ooze a juice./It has no rind being entirely hard' (*Brides of Reason*).

   Davie's redefininition of the Movement is interesting for his remarks about publicity. See 'Remembering the Movement' in Barry Alpert (ed.), *The Poet in the Imaginary Museum* (Manchester: Carcanet Press, 1977), p. 74.

For further information on the Movement style and the group's attitudes towards the 1940s, see Blake Morrison, *The Movement* (Oxford: Oxford University Press, 1980).

2. Robert Hewison, *Under Siege* (London: Weidenfeld & Nicolson, 1977) p. 113.

3. See Paul C. Ray, *The Surrealist Movement in England* (Ithaca: Cornell University Press, 1971) p. 289. Also see G. S. Fraser, *The Modern Writer and His World* (London: Derek Verschoyle, 1953) p. 267. Also Francis Scarfe, *Auden and After* (London: George Routledge, 1942) pp. 145–68. Scarfe's book is a particularly important historical document, for it charted trends and analyzed individuals of the 1930s and early 1940s in 1941–2. 'Until then', Howard Sergeant recalled in conversation, 'No one had really put on paper the attitudes of different poets. He was speaking for us and defining for us'. Personal interview with Howard Sergeant, 7 July 1980.

4. Stephen Spender, 'Some Observations on English Poetry Between Two Wars', in Stefan Schimanski and Henry Treece (eds), *Transformation 3* (London: Lindsay Drummond, n.d.) p. 3.

5. G. S. Fraser, *The Modern Writer and His World*, p. 262.

6. Henry Treece, *Dylan Thomas* (New York: John de Graff, 1956) p. 23.

7. Personal interview with John Heath-Stubbs, 8 November 1979.

8. Robin Skelton (ed.), *The Complete Poems of David Gascoyne* (Oxford: Oxford University Press, 1965) p. xi.

9. Herbert Read, 'Surrealism and the Romantic Principle', *Introduction to Surrealism* (1936), reprinted in *Selected Writings* (London: Faber & Faber, 1963) p. 282.

10. Herbert Read, 'The New Romantic School', *The Listener*, 23 April 1942, p. 533.

11. G. S. Fraser in J. F. Hendry and Henry Treece (eds), *The White Horseman* (London: Routledge, 1941) p. 3.

12. Personal interview with G. S. Fraser, 6 November 1979.

13. J. F. Hendry, as quoted in Scarfe, *Auden and After*, p. 158.

14. Treece, *Dylan Thomas*, p. 23.

15. John Goodland, letter to Henry Treece, 15 October 1938, unpublished and in private hands, quoted by Richard Helmstadter, 'The Apocalyptic Movement in British Poetry', dissertation, University of Pennsylvania, 1963, p. 18.

16. Scarfe, *Auden and After*, p. 155.

17. Henry Treece, personal interview with Richard Helmstadter, 10 August 1961.

18. Samuel Hynes, *The Auden Generation* (London: Bodley Head, 1976) pp. 94–5 and 163–4. Hynes notes the previous generation's search for heroes. Lawrence was important to them too, but as a rebel and ideologist who diagnosed the disease of the times and criticized his society.

19. J. F. Hendry, letter to Henry Treece, quoted by Helmstadter, 'The Apocalyptic Movement', p. 10. Other important influences included the Elizabethans, Donne, Kafka.

20. Geoffrey Bullough, *The Trend of Modern Poetry* (Edinburgh: Oliver and Boyd, 2nd edition, 1941) p. 159.

21. Scarfe, *Auden and After*, p. 126.

22. George Barker, 'The Miracle of Images', in John Lehmann (ed.), *Orpheus* 2 (London: John Lehmann, 1949) p. 135.
23. The Oxford circle included Charles Williams, C. S. Lewis, and J. R. R. Tolkien. See Roger Sale's essay 'England's Parnassus', *Hudson Review*, XVII, no. 2 (Summer, 1964) pp. 203–25. The three were 'not identified with each other before the war'. Williams moved to Oxford in 1939.
24. Charles Williams, quoted in Treece, *Dylan Thomas*, p. 48.
25. Dylan Thomas, letter to Henry Treece, 23 March 1938, in Constantine FitzGibbon (ed.), *The Selected Letters of Dylan Thomas* (London: Dent, 1966) pp. 190–1.
26. Treece, *Dylan Thomas*, p. 49. The essay was also printed as 'Gerard Manley Hopkins and Dylan Thomas', in Henry Treece, *How I See Apocalypse* (London: Lindsay Drummond, 1946) pp. 129–39.
27. Derek Stanford, *Inside the Forties* (London: Sidgwick & Jackson, 1977) pp. 24–26; 136.
28. Treece, *How I See Apocalypse*, p. 10.
29. Stephen Spender, *The Thirties and After* (New York: Random House, 1978) p. 72.
30. Norman Nicholson, *Man and Literature* (London: SCM Press, 1943) p. 214.
31. Norman Nicholson, *An Anthology of Religious Verse* (Harmondsworth: Penguin Books, 1942) p. IX.
32. Hewison, *Under Siege*, pp. 101–8.
33. *TLS*, 6 September 1941.
34. *TLS*, 16 May 1942.
35. Personal interview with G. S. Fraser, 6 November 1979.
36. D. J. Enright, 'Ruins and Warnings', *Scrutiny*, Summer 1942, pp. 79–80.
37. John Singer, review, *Poetry Quarterly*, Summer 1945, pp. 37–8.
38. G. S. Fraser, 'Toward Completeness', *Seven*, no. 8, Spring 1940, pp. 27–37.
39. G. S. Fraser, *Leaves Without a Tree* (Tokyo: Hokuseido Press, 1953) Preface.
40. Henry Treece and Stefan Schimanski (eds), *Transformation* (London: Victor Gollancz, 1943) pp. 13–14.
41. Henry Treece and Stefan Schimanski (eds), *A New Romantic Anthology* (London: Grey Walls Press, 1949) p. 17.
42. Dylan Thomas, letter to Richard Church, quoted by Constantine FitzGibbon, *The Life of Dylan Thomas* (Boston: Little Brown, 1965) pp. 173–4.
43. Dylan Thomas, letter to Henry Treece, 23 March 1938, as quoted by Treece, *Dylan Thomas*, p. 37. Also in FitzGibbon (ed.), *Selected Letters of Dylan Thomas*, pp. 190–91.
44. Ray, *The Surrealist Movement*, p. 280.
45. Lita Hornick, 'The Intricate Image', dissertation, Columbia University, 1958, as quoted by Ray, pp. 282–3.
46. Treece, *Dylan Thomas*, p. 56 and see p. 76.
47. Dylan Thomas, letter to John Goodland, unpublished and in private hands, quoted by Helmstadter, 'The Apocalyptic Movement', p. 24.
48. Dylan Thomas, letter to Henry Treece, 31 December 1938, in FitzGibbon (ed.), *Selected Letters of Dylan Thomas*, pp. 290–1.
49. George Orwell, *Life and Letters To-day*, June 1940, p. 315.
50. George Orwell, letter to Rayner Heppenstall, 11 April 1940, *Collected Essays, Journalism and Letters* (New York: Harcourt Brace, 1968) p. 19.

51. Dylan Thomas, letter to Henry Treece, 19 May 1938, in FitzGibbon (ed.), *Selected Letters of Dylan Thomas*, p. 196.
52. See Vernon Watkins' remarks on himself and on Thomas in John Press, *Rule and Energy* (Oxford: Oxford University Press, 1963) p. 68.
53. Stephen Spender, 'Poetry for Poetry's Sake', *Horizon*, XIII, 1946, pp. 234–5. Also see G. S. Fraser, 'Dylan Thomas', *Essays on Twentieth Century Poets* (Leicester: Leicester University Press, 1977) p. 193.

3   Where are the War Poets?

'To fight without hope is to fight with grace.'
                                                    – Henry Reed

I

The poets of the First World War performed a posthumous
disservice to the poets of the Second World War. Rupert Brooke,
Julian Grenfell, Herbert Asquith, Wilfred Owen, Isaac Rosenberg, Siegfried Sassoon and others less well known had created
public expectations of what war poets should be. Immediately
upon the outbreak of war in August 1914, Rupert Brooke had
issued a 'trumpet call' – soon followed by the productions of other
young writers – declaring that a new spirit of heroism could now
replace the 'sickness' of the 'pre-1914 world'.[1] No such outburst of
spirit was evident by the time of the Dunkirk evacuation in May
1940. Still, the British public steadfastly continued to associate
poetry with war. An article entitled 'To the Poets of 1940',
appended to a review of the year's poetry in the *TLS* of 30
December 1939, called upon poets in wartime to rise to the
occasion once again: 'Here we are faced with an undeniable
repetition of history, with nothing original, nothing unique about
it. Clearly wars and revolutions are destroying the old social order
of the world. But we need not despair of the birth of a new and
finer order. It is for the poets to sound the trumpet call'.[2]
    In their summons for war poetry, editors and reviewers were
remembering those early poets of the Great War who had been
nationalistic spokesmen for the people.[3] Even Stephen Spender,
who carefully dissociated the 1939–40 war poets from all earlier
ones, urged them to assert the 'strength of a faith in civilization
which will be able to conquer and survive' and to capture in verse
the 'society of the future'.[4] The poets of the Second World War
were expected to lead the way in uniting England spiritually and

52

socially just as Brooke, Grenfell and Asquith had before them. It was assumed that the second generation of war poets would also write for a national audience.

When the call went out in 1939 for a public poetry and for 'optimistic songs of deliverance', Rupert Brooke came to mind first as the poet who had embodied such nationalism.[5] Brooke and those who shared his beliefs were responsible for the myth of 1914, a myth of traditional Empire, self-assurance, and a hopeful future. In battle for England, Brooke found a chance to express the values he had grown up with in the drawing room and on the playing field: duty, honour, nobility. War could provide the exciting opportunity to be a hero and the chance to create a better world. Even as late as 1942, Brooke continued to be evoked. Though nationalistic verse was not in fashion, the populace and journalists still required a sacrificial boy-poet, an honour they mistakenly conferred on the dead Sidney Keyes.[6]

Such enthusiasm could not be duplicated for very long in 1939–40. And when the poets of the Second World War themselves turned back to models, they most often recalled not Brooke, but the ironic and compassionate realists of the trenches: Wilfred Owen, Isaac Rosenberg and Siegfried Sassoon. When poets of the second generation recalled the first, they did so not to join a tradition, but to differentiate themselves. For the war of 1939–45 did not resemble the Great War in kind.

The Second World War did not immediately produce outstanding 'war poets', and the nature of the war partly explains why. In the autumn and winter of 1939, England and Germany were officially at war but no actual fighting began until spring 1940 when Hitler's armies marched on Belgium and Holland. Until then, this 'phoney war' created a strained and unreal atmosphere in England. Starting as a war of nerves, the Second World War stunned the imagination instead of liberating it. There was no development from initial optimism about war to rejection of it, a development clearly evident in the poetry of the First World War. Furthermore in the Second World War the contrast between trench warfare and the Edenic English countryside at home was not as pronounced. No myths of pastoral retreats gathered around the Second War. Like a cancer, war gradually spread to a wide series of fronts. As Stephen Spender said, it had 'no stage setting easily visualized'.[7]

The armed forces of the Second World War were also different.

In the beginning of the Great War volunteers had led the way to the front. Not until 1917 did a Conscription Act force men to fight for England and thereby cancel the choice of being a hero voluntarily. Unlike the eager patriots of 1914, few men sought the adventure of war in 1939. The poet H. B. Mallalieu summed up the attitude of his generation: 'The necessity of war was accepted and if the challenge was not accepted with the jubilation that Rupert Brooke had shown . . . it was seen as inevitable'.[8] The conscripts joined armed services where nearly all the senior officers were professionals. As Robert Graves reported in a 1941 article on War Poetry, 'even its newest battalions are anything but ragtime; and it is being increasingly mechanised'.[9] Resignation settled over the enthusiasm of 1914.

Individual heroism, possible in hand-to-hand combat of the Great War, was not absent in 1940; yet the increased mechanization of this war often meant less personal investment. Whole countries fell at the mercy of the battle machine. More than ever before, aeroplanes, submarines and tanks prevented personal contact betwen the British and their foes. Responding to these different conditions, the poets of the Second World War encountered an isolation so intense that it often crushed the creative spirit. Reviewing a group of younger poets in 1943, Clifford Dyment used the phrase, 'these poets are less critics of war than prisoners of war'.[10] *Dulled, bored, dead* – such words recur often in the poetry of the Second World War poets. Roy Fuller finds no easy identification with his role of war poet in 'The Middle of a War' where 'His fate [is] so obviously preordained':

> My photograph already looks historic
> The promising youthful face, the matelot collar
> Say 'This one is remembered for a lyric.
> His place and period – nothing could be duller.'

Like all soldiers, the poets faced a death that was imminent yet at the same time fearfully abstract. Alan Rook records common feelings in 'Dunkirk Pier' (1942):

> why should this lark
> exploring extinction and oneness of self and air
> remind us that, lonely and lost as flowers in deserted

weed-mastered gardens, each faint face averted
from the inescapable confusion, for each of us slowly
death on his last, most hideous journey has started?

Anti-heroic, the poets of the Second World War did not assume
the role of prophets either. Donald Bain's 'War Poet' is a private
poet: 'We in our haste can only see the small components of the
scene'.

While the 'intimacy' of the First World War had to a large
degree vanished, such a deep separation between soldiers abroad
and civilians in England no longer existed. For the blitz claimed
thousands of victims. The tank driver at El Alamein could not be
sure that his family in Coventry was as safe as it had been in
1914–18. Totally controlling the landscape, the machines of war
spurred British poets and artists located across the globe to
emphasize the personal and distinctly human. In the introduction
to his 1966 Penguin anthology *Components of the Scene*, Ronald
Blythe spoke of the centrality of the self in a war with no fixed
geographical limits: 'Each poet spoke as wholly and truthfully as
he could from out of the one inviolable spot of an otherwise
violated order, his own identity'.[11]

The best poetry of 1939–45 was unlike the socially-oriented
poetry British journalists had at first summoned. Anti-heroic and
anti-rhetorical, the 1940s poets took a bleak approach to war.
Many shared Roy Fuller's sense of community: 'My living now
must bear the laceration / of the herd, and always will. What's
done / To me is done to many:' ('What is Terrible'). Yet most
often, they illuminated the common lot through their own
personal trials. Sidney Keyes' 'War Poet' blames fate or history
for forcing him into the ways of battle: 'I am the man who looked
for peace and found / My own eyes barbed. I am the man who
groped for words and found / An arrow in my hand'.

Some poets, conscious of their predecessors' work, acknow-
ledged openly that they could not write a poetry of nationalism or
of World War violence. Gavin Ewart stressed the war as only a
background to his individual experience: 'Personally I feel very
strongly that the best poems about war (modern war) have
already been written – most of them by Wilfred Owen before he
died in 1918. In a good many cases, all we can do today is to
rewrite the poems of the earlier war. All we can do is to provide

footnotes, the small, detailed cameos of our own experience'.[12]
Keith Douglas' bow to Isaac Rosenberg in his poem 'Desert
Flowers' (1943) similarly compliments the earlier generation but
also indicates the acceptance of a personal mission:

Desert Flowers

Living in a wide landscape are the flowers –
Rosenberg I only repeat what you were saying –
the shell and the hawk every hour
are slaying men and jerboas, slaying

the mind: but the body can fill
the hungry flowers and the dogs who cry words
at nights, the most hostile things of all.
But that is not new. Each time the night discards

draperies on the eyes and leaves the mind awake
I look each side of the door of sleep
for the little coin it will take
to buy the secret I shall not keep.

I see men as trees suffering
or confound the detail and the horizon.
Lay the coin on my tongue and I will sing
of what others never set eyes on.

Because the later war was so different, it compelled poets to
envision war afresh. In the Second World War there were various
kinds of 'war poetry': poetry of battle, poetry of exile, anti-war
poetry, and much verse written (like that of Edward Thomas)
against the background of war, but not necessarily about war.
These poets, like those before them, were speaking for a generation, yet they held few illusions. 'To trust anyone or to admit any
hope of a better world', wrote Douglas to J. C. Hall three years into
the war, 'is as criminally foolish as it is to stop working for it'.[13]
Mildred Davidson has succinctly characterized the major difference between poets of the First and Second World Wars: 'Rupert
Brooke had idealised the things he loved as worth dying for. The
second generation of war poets wanted to possess those things

once again before they died. Their poetry is a history of the struggle to retain and the struggle to give up'.[14] In this light, Alun Lewis best presents that special conflict of the Second World War poet: 'Acceptance seems so spiritless, protest so vain. In between the two I live'.[15]

Poets of the Second World War, bred to face death, can be fixed as having been born between 1914 and 1922, though inevitably there are major exceptions. This grouping would include men and women who were born during the First World War and those who either started university or came of age in 1939. The common experiences of war drew these young people together and defined their generation; yet the keynote of the 1940s was one of personal expression. Some were overwhelmed by the chaos around them, some felt their identities threatened or lost as they played out roles in a cosmic drama. Almost all of them, like Lewis, walked the fine line between active participation and the detachment necessary for sanity.

II

Examining the Oxford scene during the early years of war, one finds the same division of interest among the literati who were expected to become the successors of Auden. 'Our generation', John Heath-Stubbs said recently, 'metaphorically spat at Brooke'.[16] Brooke's typically naive patriotism could hold no meaning for the young poets of the early forties. It interfered with more important and enduring interests: love, art, and for some, the pleasures of university life. As war stole their youth, so it also destroyed the intellectual communities which might have served their common aims. Tutorials were given by the older dons; young friends were progressively called up, many never to return. Poets like Keith Douglas, Sidney Keyes, Drummond Allison, John Heath-Stubbs, and later Philip Larkin and Kingsley Amis were tentatively organizing themselves: starting up anthologies, meeting in pubs, sharing ideas about poetry, writing together for *The Cherwell* or other literary magazines. Yet the groups, if they can be termed so at all, dispersed almost as soon as they were formed.

While Cambridge nurtured the talents of poets such as Donald

Bain, Alex Comfort, Gavin Ewart, Nicholas Moore, John Bayliss, and later, Donald Davie, the more interesting group productions happened to be at Oxford; and Oxford bred many of the best poets of the decade to follow. While Oxford publications flourished, Cambridge's literary magazines did not fare terribly well during the war years. John Lehmann recalls journeying to Cambridge with poets from Oxford in the early 1940s in an attempt to organize an Oxbridge magazine.[17] But the project failed and only one number of the new periodical 'Z' (now lost, as far as I can trace it) was published. John Heath-Stubbs and John Lehmann account for the failed union by suggesting that Cambridge had 'had her day' in the twenties and thirties – now it was Oxford's turn.[18]

The young men came up to Oxford when the university was understaffed. Arts faculties were reduced to a quarter of pre-war strength. In the first years of war, arts students were able to stay until the age of 20, but when the conscription age was lowered to 18, most of the new students were women, or men unfit for service.[19] For all, it meant an interrupted life.

Not only had the traditional make-up of Oxford changed, but the tenor of life differed considerably from pre-war years. In his 1963 retrospective preface to *Jill*, Philip Larkin described wartime Oxford. The city was, he wrote, 'singularly free from . . . traditional (social) distinctions. Undergraduates liable for service could expect three or four terms at most' (one full year or a year and a term).[20] The old college and university rituals, such as the annual commemoration balls, were suspended. Dress was more sober; not many students ran cars. In *The Heat of the Day*, Elizabeth Bowen drew such an aborted life in her character Roderick: 'he had expected neutrally, to become a soldier; he was a soldier now. To his year at Oxford there had been denied meaning'.[21] Of Oxford in 1942, Michael Howard remembers hunting for the simple pleasures between drills in the Meadows: 'We had a bottle of sherry a term from the buttery, and queued in the town for cakes and for whatever nauseating concoction we could extract from the wine-merchants'.[22]

This generation of fledgling Oxford poets, born too early or too late, knew when they went up to university that the stay would be brief; yet they felt it was important to document their feelings. A 'Wartime Letter' published in *Oxford and Cambridge Writing* (1942) by Roland Loewe, captures well their discouraged sense of

emporal displacement while reaffirming their need to contri-
bute: 'We feel we haven't the time to achieve anything permanent
and yet we don't want to die without adding our bit of muck to the
general dung heap. . . . Perhaps there are among us real poets and
. . good writers, so that, what is said now, however unimportant
intrinsically, is worth saying to make a beginning'.[23]

Throughout the poems and articles published in Oxford
magazines runs a double strain – the uneasy desire for perfor-
mance and a bitterness about separation. As early as January
1939, these intellectuals wrote their own epitaphs. A short story
by the poet and editor John Waller, for instance, portrayed the
imagined devastation of Oxford by enemy forces (Oxford's
destruction, feared by many, was never a possibility in the mind of
Hitler, who planned to set up a government there). 'Massacre in
the High' describes fascist planes converging on the city of
dreaming spires and demolishing it:

> The first air-raid came over at midday on the third morning of
> the siege. About fifty planes came flying over from Port
> Meadow, dropping bombs on those fine edifices. The Bodleian
> went, so did the Camera and Sheldonian, St. Mary's and
> Magdalen Tower. The machine guns in the cockpit poured
> their rain of bullets into the High. Thousands that day were
> killed in the streets.[24]

This article grotesquely satirizes the deaths of dons, librarians
and students with humorous abandon. It also documents the fear
of real apocalypse.

Published in the same issue, an anonymous poem called 'Crisis'
expresses standard fears – the loss of a lover through faithlessness,
shock in battle, scarring wounds:

> Dearest, when the bombs begin to fall,
> Will you or I be here at all?
> Will the peace-time picture in its civilian frame
> Ever again look quite the same?

Neutral, resentful, fearful, angry: all these adjectives can be applied
to the generation of 1939 at Oxford. But their equally fervent
determination to keep the traditions of Oxford alive is reflected in
a continuously active social life. As might be expected, political

groups were eagerly supported. The Labour Club had split into two parts: Marxists and Social Democrats. In lively Union debates students voted no confidence in the government (26 November 1938) and for abolition of the press (14 November 1940). Music too seemed to thrive under wartime conditions. *The Cherwell* run of the period indicates that during any given week one laboured to decide among subscription concerts, organ recitals, productions of the Musical Union, Oxford Ladies' Club activities, and university concerts. Plays were eagerly produced and well-attended. Though with the war's blackouts and food rationing university life had lost its earlier grace and loveliness, students tried to make the best of it.

Young poets remained very active as well. It is tempting to focus on the best poets immediately, whose who ran the magazines or were quietly forging reputations. But a look at versifiers in Oxford helps put the poets into better perspective. The following typical stanzas, one blatantly anti-political and one politically-oriented, reflect the oscillation between involvement and detachment felt by the Oxford youth. Both poems were published in *Kingdom Come, the Magazine of Wartime Oxford* in Autumn 1940.

The Forest Pool

Don't you remember Gösta? It was high
Summer: we had been tramping the whole day
Through forests when a tarn got in our way
Among clouds – don't you remember how they lay
Among the lotuses like fantastic feathers
Dropped by a bird of legend in the twi-
Lit nest of evening? How we cried out together,
Threw off our clothes and dived into the sky.

(Terence Heywood)

For Denmark – 1940

The boulder sand and lignite formed
The Athlete's arm of Denmark, shaped
A muscular peninsula
Guarding the Baltic and the West.
And taut the muscles, sinews, nerves,

(The will of Gruntwig and of God)
Lifted this arm in constant prayer
To avert the wrath of a just God.

(John Short)

The poems printed in the Oxford magazines of the period, those by versifiers and those by poets, easily reveal the poetic influences on this generation. David Guest in 'Poem' (*The Cherwell*, 14 November 1940) owes a strong debt to Auden: 'And we shall lie beneath the tree / Offending no morality, / Nor need to hesitate to prove / Existence of a mutual love'. At another extreme, John Heath-Stubbs uses almost surrealistic images in 'Simile': 'just as the cormorant (with stretched out throttle / And glossed green plumage), shaped like a beer-bottle, / Flaps heavily across the qualmish sea, / With splay feet dangling down'. Eliot and Yeats acted as prime models. Roy Porter's 'Walk to Departure', published in *Eight Oxford Poets*, for instance, echoes *The Waste Land*:

The white girl said 'Leb' wohl
Ewig, ewig.
. . .

I am weary of heavy thinking
Of discovery and striving
Of comparison and judging
That is the substance of thought.
. . .

But you looked back behind me into the wood
To an hour ago and to infinity concentrating
End and beginning, turned even from yourself;
Which is the faith I do not understand.

Early poems by both Larkin and Keyes (poets who would develop in totally different directions) reflect a common heritage in Yeats:

Butterfly

or falling leaf,
Which ought I to imitate
In my dancing?
And if she were to admit
The world weaved by her feet
Is leafless, is incomplete?

      (Philip Larkin in 'The Dancer' from *The North Ship*)

Spirit-bodies loveliness
Cannot expiate my pain:
How should I learn wisdom
Being old and profane?

      (Sidney Keyes, 'William Yeats in Limbo' from
      Collected Poems)

Though Auden, Eliot, Yeats and Dylan Thomas stimulated the young, influences most often combined as the new poets sought their own subjects and voices.

    There was one poet, however, who figured as an important ideological influence for some members of this generation – Rainer Maria Rilke. In Rilke they found a mind congenial to their own situation and they were attracted to his intense sensuality.[25] Auden had borrowed from Rilke for his own ends, but the new poets were drawn to his notion that man carries his own death within him. A stanza from one of the *Duino Elegies*[26] illustrates his concern with man's consciousness of death:

only see death; the free animal
has its decrease perpetually behind it
and God in front, and when it moves, it moves
into eternity, like running springs.
We've never, no, not for a single day,
pure space before us, such as that which flowers
endlessly open into; always world
and never nowhere without no: that pure
unsuperintended element one breathes,
endlessly knows, and never craves.

The notion of death-in-life was of central concern to a neo-romantic poet such as Sidney Keyes whose allurement towards death matched his repulsion from it. Rilke's popularity magnified tremendously during the early 1940s because of Leishman's translations published by the Hogarth Press and Stephen Spender's articles, such as 'The Influence of Rilke on English Poetry' (*The Listener*, 18 July 1946). Directly enlarging the awareness of other poets, Rilke did not simply provide a storehouse for borrowings. Perhaps it is in keeping with the internationalism of the middle 1940s that a 'foreign' poet made such a profound impact. But his influence would not have been so great if several generations of British poets were not already withdrawing from social concerns to confront metaphysical and private questions.

The best poets at Oxford during 1940–42 were scattered among the various men's colleges. The pugnacious and brilliant Keith Douglas was at Merton, Francis King was at Balliol, David Wright at Oriel, John Mortimer at Brasenose; the others seem to fall conveniently into two main centres. The reserved and intellectual neo-romantics at Queen's included John Heath-Stubbs and Sidney Keyes. Their talented friend Drummond Allison was also there. Alan Ross and Philip Larkin were at St Johns by 1940–41; Kingsley Amis came up in the summer term of 1941 to the college that would welcome a third 'Movement' member in 1943: John Wain. At one time, Keyes, Heath-Stubbs, Larkin and Allison were all at Oxford. Keith Douglas may have overlapped by a month or two, but he left in June 1940.

Two 'circles' seemed to be forming, one neo-romantic, erudite in its allusions and metaphysical in its concerns, the other more formal, derivative from Yeats and Auden and lagging a bit in productions behind the first. While Philip Larkin and Kingsley Amis developed more slowly and were possibly irritated by the dominating Queen's group, Larkin has said recently that there was 'no college rivalry'.[27] There may well have been some personal rivalry, however. For while Keyes admired Larkin's work, he chose not to include it in the important anthology he edited with Michael Meyer of Christ Church: *Eight Oxford Poets*. John Heath-Stubbs has alluded to an unspoken jealousy between the two groups that would later flourish in the poetry of two decades. In a 1978 interview with G. H. B. Wightman, Heath-Stubbs reappraised the poetry scene in the early forties at Oxford:

Anybody who was known to write poetry in the university tended to get drawn into that circle (Queen's). But some held aloof, and I now realize rather deliberately held aloof and disapproved. That was the Amis/Larkin circle at St John's.[28]

Though Larkin himself showed many of the trappings of romanticism in his early verse, he apparently held an anti-romantic attitude from the start; likewise, Heath-Stubbs believes Amis' later poem 'Against Romanticism' is a deliberate slur against the kinds of images found in the poems of Sidney Keyes. Larkin's stunned reactions to these poets are recorded in his retrospective (1965) preface to *The North Ship*. There he noted with some coyness:

> I remember looking through an isssue of *The Cherwell*, one day in Blackwell's, and coming across John Heath-Stubbs' 'Leporello': I was profoundly bewildered. I had never heard of Leporello, and what sort of poetry was this – who was he copying? And his friend Sidney Keyes was no more comforting: he could talk to history as some people talk to porters, and the mention of names like Schiller and Rilke and Gilles de Retz made me wish I were reading something more demanding than English Language and Literature.[29]

The great gap that Larkin felt between himself and these other poets is nicely symbolized by his memory of Keyes stopping to speak to him in the Turl. Larkin recalled, 'I suppose we must have known each other to talk to – that is, if we had anything to say. As far as I remember, we hadn't'.[30]

The poet who stands apart from any identifiable group, and who seems to have preferred his separateness was Keith Douglas. At Oxford 1938–40, Douglas missed the acquaintance of Larkin and Amis. While Douglas probably knew Keyes from their work for *The Cherwell*, there is no record of their meeting, and Douglas had already gone into the army when Keyes commissioned poems for the Oxford anthology he edited in 1941. Yet Douglas was an important literary figure at Oxford during the two years he was there. In 1940, Edmund Blunden (his tutor), Alec Hardie and Douglas produced an anthology called *Augury*, a collection most interesting as a social document, especially when compared with Sidney Keyes' plan for an anthology of a year later.

While *Augury*, published as a stay against war, remained nostalgically committed to the past or future, *Eight Oxford Poets* sought to define a new poetic generation for the present. Douglas' preface to *Augury* does not confront war directly but forces it into the background: 'The nature of the poetry in this volume is not nearly so introspective or gloomy as might have been feared. The poets in this anthology are not with the times, but in most of their thoughts hark back or forward to a better age'.[31] Douglas' own poems in *Augury* evoke an older stabler world.[32] In 'Villanelle of Spring Bells', he praises the natural forces of beauty that can 'banish cares':

> All evil men intent on evil thing
> falter, for in their cold unready ears
> bells in the town alight with spring
> make clear the fresh and ancient sound they sing.

'Pas de Trois' tells of three dancer-deities who lived in a world of pure pleasure:

> Theirs is a craft of quiet
> They are shades of an old time
> When you could hear no riot
> intervening, intricate and frail rhyme
> and music;

With his contribution 'Haydn – Military Symphony', Douglas undercuts the military with memories of a more eternal music. 'Yet scrutinizing the regimental pair / and you will find, they are but men of air.' The eternal soldiers are insubstantial, yet more real to Douglas than all the troops at war in 1940.

If *Augury* was an important statement of Oxford's desire to preserve the simple and lasting aspects of human life against the threat of destruction, *Eight Oxford Poets*, which sold out in three weeks, proved to be the most important poetic manifesto of the Oxbridge war years. Instead of relying on memories or desires, Keyes (who wrote the preface) examined the present situation, the inevitability of destruction, and the need for a new vision. Larkin professed in 1964 that 'following *Eight Oxford Poets*, Oxford poetry was reputedly on the ascendant again'.[33] Recalled by Michael Meyer as 'the most exciting literary figure of my time at Oxford',[34] Keyes made final decisions about contributors and poems. Meyer, who helped Keyes with some selections, has recounted the conception and execution of the anthology as follows:[35]

> In 1941, Keyes and I compiled an anthology entitled *Eight Oxford Poets*, containing work by him and me, Heath-Stubbs, Allison, Keith Douglas, Roy Porter, Gordon Swaine and J. A. Shaw. I say 'Keyes and I' but it was he who did the choosing, and I am not sure why he asked me to co-edit with him – probably, I now think, out of a polite desire not to seem to be by-passing his *Cherwell* editor. I know we disagreed considerably about who should be in. I wanted to include Larkin, among others, and was still dubious about Heath-Stubbs and Allison. In the end he had his way, and I think, apart from Larkin, that he was right.

Eight Oxford Poets was the first attempt by the new generation to establish a poetic platform. In the introduction, a manifesto for a new school of poetry, Keyes wrote: 'We are all, with the possible exception of Shaw, "Romantic" writers, though by that I mean little more than that our greatest fault is a tendency to floridity; and that we have, on the whole, little sympathy with the Audenian school of poets'.[36] Keyes was promoting a new romanticism, but one unlike Surrealism or Apocalyptic poetry. In his desire to unite the poets into a 'school', Keyes called the anthology a 'group production', but his assertion was not true. The contributors were not involved in the making of the book, nor did they share common poetic theories. Keith Douglas, for instance, had little or no control over his own contributions. In 1941 he wrote to his friend Margaret Stanley-Wrench: 'I had nothing to do with the compiling of it . . . Michael Meyer chose which of my poems to include'.[37] Drummond Allison, who was to produce only one (posthumous) volume of poetry, *The Yellow Night* (1944), was definitely influenced by Auden. In the recent limited edition of his *Poems*, Michael Sharp has noted: 'Allison, who strangely assented to Keyes' claim in the [anthology's] introduction that none of the poets had any sympathy for the Auden school of poetry, managed to make at least one critic notice the debt in technique he himself owed to Auden'.[38] Keyes' remarks, in the introduction, were purposely general in order to 'create' a group that did not exist. They described Heath-Stubbs and himself best. As Robert Hewison has remarked: these two young men were 'evolving a metaphysical poetry that explored man's psychological states through myth and symbol'.[39] Their literary interests were the same: Blake, Yeats, Wordsworth and Rilke, but they did not have a large group of followers.

Another part of the introduction to *Eight Oxford Poets*, where Keyes also betrays his desire for all-inclusiveness, is more applicable to the poets as a group. He described 'certain elements common to us all' – 'We seem to share a horror at the world's predicament, together with the feeling that we cannot save ourselves without some kind of spiritual readjustment, though the nature of that readjustment may take widely differing forms'.[40] Within Keyes' rubric of 'horror' and 'spiritual readjustment', the eight Oxford poets remained individual voices.

Taken together, *Augury* and *Eight Oxford Poets* characterize the double interest of the university-trained poets who were facing war, a bifurcated vision that they would share with many other poets in the Forces. Their poetry betrays both the need to retain an old self and way of life and the willingness to search for meaning elsewhere.

It is easy enough to so categorize the young poets at Oxford; yet all were still fledglings in the process of casting off older influences, and no single group emerged from the Oxford of 1939–42. The time to establish common ground was cut short. For many poets, their first volume of verse was their last, while others went on to establish individual reputations.

In his 'Wartime Letter', quoted earlier, Loewe was largely pessimistic about the future of Oxbridge poetry because of the haunting spectre of death: 'And if there is no one among us, who will stand out to be remembered, then it will have been worthwhile to record what young men felt and thought'. In fact, the poets emerging from this Oxford matrix proved themselves worthy of individual remembrance. John Heath-Stubbs, Philip Larkin, Michael Meyer, Kingsley Amis and others developed in separate directions during and after the war. Drummond Allison, unjustly forgotten, died at twenty-two after only six weeks of active service in Italy. Sidney Keyes and Keith Douglas went on to establish themselves as the two finest English poets of the war years.

III

From 1939 to 1945 hundreds of men and women in military or government service wrote poetry. Writing out of the extreme conditions of exile, fear, isolation and danger, they made their way into print via Forces magazines now long forgotten. Many of their productions were immature, hastily written and sentimental. Much deserves the dust that has accumulated over it. However, not all was third or second rate. The best poets include Keith Douglas, Sidney Keyes, Alun Lewis, Roy Fuller, Alan Ross, Henry Reed, Lawrence Durrell, Gavin Ewart, Bernard Spencer, Terence Tiller and G. S. Fraser.

In retrospect, it is important that thousands of people were writing poetry at all; the lyric of personal experience seemed to provide the best way to make sense of so terrible and abstract a holocaust. Peter Ratazzi, editing the armed forces publication *Khaki and Blue*, described the outpouring of verse. The forces were reading and discussing literature as never before: 'To us younger poets and writers in battledress – it (the anthology) is in effect an act of faith'.[41] Ratazzi went on to describe the positive value of writing outside of traditional literary circles:

> We cannot attain the high quality of a Sidney Keyes or an Alun Lewis (young writers recently killed on active service overseas); but together away from anaemic scribble – cliques and aesthetic-eclectic frondes – and out of the experience of the whole of a people we can record and interpret – even in a modest anthology like our own – the issues confronting and shaping the future and fate of our bewildering time.

Ratazzi's vision of writing poetry as an act of faith was not unique.

While the London literary circles and publications such as *Horizon* were closed to the average poet, certain individuals helped promote armed forces poetry. *Poems from the Forces*, an anthology edited by Kiedrych Rhys, was enormously popular. John Lehmann did more singlehandedly for service poets with his *Penguin New Writing* than any other major editor. His little magazine was the most popular among the troops. Other major anthologies included: *Poems from India, Poems from Italy, Poems from France, Poems from Cambridge, Poetry from Oxford in Wartime*, and *Air Force Poetry*.

Such a selective list informs us of the quantity of forums for poetry, but gives us no indication of the poets' reactions to war. For Douglas Grant, who wrote a retrospective essay 'War and the Writer'[42] war inspired fear but also excitement. He opposed the dull domestic routine of peacetime to the 'increased consciousness' of wartime. 'Each sense', he wrote, 'which peace and its dull living had jaded demands delight.' For others, like Gavin Ewart, 'Writing Poetry during the war was very hard. The war itself, as a subject was too near and too big'.[43]

Most poets wrote, at some point or other, of the stupidity of war and of their confusion. Denton Welch in 'Rural Raid', describes all the countryside he can see as dull endless flame: 'Only the sudden metal weight of fear / Brings back the platitude that life is dear, / Keeps us awake while we sit staring out / With Reason pounding, "What's it all about?" ' In 'Embarkation Song', Geoffrey Matthews has not yet approached Welch's bitterness, yet he too feels the aimlessness of the war: 'I'm joking, dear; and I shan't ask what you're doing / While I'm abroad, or how you wait. / But quick, tell me once more why I'm going, / Before it is too late.' Perhaps Charles Causley's 'Soldiers' Chorus' is the most direct anti-war statement: 'Say that you did it for glory / Defending your hoary name / It's still the same bloody old story / And I'm pushed in the pit just the same'. Forced into a war they did not want, these poets rarely resorted to outright satire. Few even identified closely with the enemy (Keith Douglas is one of the major exceptions). Often in the face of death they chose to write lyrically of life:

It is Death Now We Look Upon

Dayfall
swallowsong,
murmurous the river
which is memory –

it is death we now look upon.

Wherefore call home the old
and let them lie
lapped in their shaken
yet unshaken, faith;

> call home tomorrow's quick
> the beautiful, the glad
> the unrelenting.
>
> Call home the children
> we have made
> but shall not know.
>
>   . . .
>
> it is death now we look upon
>   (T. R. Hodgson, killed in action 1941)

Roy Fuller, whose war poetry is notable for its social awareness, often conveyed anger and pathos through irony, as in 'Epitaph on a Bombing Victim':

> Reader could his limbs be found
> Here would lie a common man:
> History inflicts no wound
> But explodes what it began
> And with its enormous lust
> For division splits the dust.
> Do not ask his nation; that
> Was History's confederate.

Roy Fuller was one of the few poets who rode out the storms of war and developed because of them. Born somewhat earlier than the generation we have defined, in 1912, he was an imitator of the Auden group as well as a Marxist sympathizer before war broke out. Following Auden, he had written typical 1930s poetry that emphasized the tensions of personal and public responsibilities, the need to create a 'simpler' poetry than that of the 1920s. His participation in the war began in the navy in 1941; in 1942 he was sent to East Africa as a radar technician for the Fleet Air Arm. Fuller has described how the war helped his poetry develop: 'War service . . . exchanged reality for illusion, and after the war, following an awkward period of adjustment, I was able to write verse of rather wider scope . . . the Marxist conception of things underlies them (the war poems) in a less strained and dragged-in way than hitherto'.[44]

Exile to East Africa was a boring and depressing experience for Fuller, yet it infused his poetry with a greater concreteness and fresh themes. He was still concerned with the relationship between the individual and society (as in 'Spring 1943') but the African landscape stimulated him to observe new details of the natural world and to connect them to the human. There is a richness to the poetry from Africa which his earlier poems lack. Fuller has said: 'War gave me a subject'[45] but it also developed his style. Selections from 'August 1938' and 'Giraffes' reveal the new vitality Fuller achieved:

August 1938

Mapping this bay and charting
The water's ribby base
By individual smarting
And walks in shifting sand,
We note the official place;
Dover with pursed-up lips
Behind the purple land
To danger, large and bland;

The Giraffe

I think before they saw me the giraffes
Were watching me. Over the golden grass,
The bush and ragged open tree of thorn
From a grotesque height, under their lightish horns,
Their eyes were fixed on mine as I approached them.

. . .

So as they put more ground between us I
Saw evidence that these were animals
With no desire for intercourse, or no
Capacity.

Above the falling sun,
Like visible winds the clouds are streaked and spun,
And cold and dark now bring the image of
Those creatures walking without pain or love.

Fuller's development towards a poetry of naturalistic detail is further illustrated by such poems as 'The Green Hills of Africa' and 'The Plains', but of greater importance is his deeper expression of human connection with a landscape. In a poem he sent to Julian Symons during the war (reprinted in Symons' book *The Thirties*), Fuller calls the Auden idiom into question: 'Oddly, I found / Last week, in a little, ancient magazine, / Some of the crabbed, uncompromising verses / We used to write. I wonder what they mean.' Fuller was exiled by war but the result was that he was thrown face to face with new subjects. He is representative as the self-educated poet who survived war – who did not develop stylistically to any great extent, but who widened his vision and learned a more authoritative voice that was not mere mimicry of Auden.

IV

During the war, foreign service enabled some poets, like Fuller, to develop talents which might have withered at home; yet the most interesting group of exiles were by far those located in Cairo, the equivalent of an eastern centre for intellectuals. The wartime expatriate class contributed heavily to the international flavour of the 1940s and to a renewed interest in topography. It was no surprise that, after the war, English poets rebelled against 'foreign' places and vowed to return to the English provincial scene. Yet in the early 1940s, when there was no dominant school of poetry, individuals could easily grow and develop, especially away from home.

The Middle East was one of the least disagreeable landscapes for exile. There, civilians joined with soldiers on leave to create a poetry of place both personal and highly descriptive. An important literary magazine called *Personal Landscape* was born in the Anglo-Egyptian Union in Cairo where men and women interested in the arts could meet and exchange ideas. Some of those who frequented the Union were: Terence Tiller, Hugh Gordon Porteous, an expert on Chinese art, Bernard Spencer, Keith Douglas, Robin Fedden, Iain Fletcher, John Gawsworth, John Waller, G. S. Fraser, Hamish Henderson, Robert Liddell and Lawrence Durrell. An anthology called *Personal Landscape*, also edited by Fedden, was published in Cairo in 1945. This magazine and its companion anthology were not the only foreign publications in the Middle East, however. Other magazines welcoming literary contributions included *Forum, Citadel, Salamander* and *Orientations*.

Writers abroad bonded quickly into a Cairo circle. These writers did not necessarily share common outlooks about poetry, but were 'united in exile',[46] as Robin Fedden said in the *Personal Landscape* anthology. He hastened to add that exile was not a tragic situation, but a stagnation of spirit. He described the difficulties that individuals shared: 'the changeless climate, the facelessness of the landscape – flat, spineless, muffled, with no rock – which forced these poets to construct landscapes of their own'.[47] Olivia Manning, also living in Cairo at this time, wrote an article about her fellow artists. In 'Poets in Exile' (*Horizon*, October 1944) she described the differences between writers in the Middle East and in England. Because manuscripts took as long as three months to reach England, artists had ceased to 'look homewards'.[48]

But these cosmopolitan writers absorbed the strange culture around them slowly. Only gradually, Olivia Manning wrote, did writers begin

> to admit in their work the curiosities and beauties of a country that, beneath its flattening, white light, offered the naked desert, the crowded lushly cultivated delta of the peasant, the filth and opulence of the towns – a country that resembled no other in the world.[49]

Fedden too noted the enormous contrasts of Egypt, a country whose cultural traditions focused on mortality: 'The exile everywhere walks on the dead and their deposits . . . the dead of countless generations, packed like sardines, stuff the earth. It bursts with corpses'.[50] He was fascinated by dissimilarities in the landscape: temples near concrete apartment blocks. *Personal Landscape*, which Fedden and Spencer edited, made two volumes (8 issues) from 1942 to 1945. For those three years it provided a forum for serious writers stationed in the Middle East. Its contents were of a high quality; a typical issue carried a translation of Rilke by Ruth Spiers, poems by Douglas ('Desert Flowers' in vol. 2, pt. 1, 'Cairo Jag' in vol. 2, pt. 2), an article on Cavafy, a poet discoursing on his own art (Durrell in vol. 2, pt. 1, Tiller in vol. 1, pt. 1).

Many fine poems that were written in Cairo, such as 'The Traveller Has Regrets' by G. S. Fraser, speak of separation and a longing for home. 'You got in the habit of looking at things differently,' Fraser has said, 'you looked at the Nile and you also used your eyes backwards, seeing what you'd left. Home itself acquired something of the exotic.'[51] 'Egypt' expresses the safe and easy life of Cairo and the bitterness of exile:

> Who knows the lights at last, who knows the cities
> And the unloving hands upon the thighs
> Would yet return to seek his home-town pretties
> For the shy finger-tips and sidelong eyes.
>
> Who knows the world, the flesh, the compromises
> Would go back to the theory in the book;
> Who knows the place the poster advertises
> Back to the poster for another look.
>
> But nets the fellah spreads beside the river
> Where the green waters criss-cross in the sun
> End certain migratory hopes for ever;
> In that white light, all shadows are undone.
>
> The desert slays. But safe from Allah's justice
> Where the broad river of His Mercy lies,
> Where ground for labour, or where scope for lust is,
> The crooked and tall and cunning cities rise.
>
> The green Nile irrigates a barren region,
> All the coarse palms are ankle-deep in sand;
> No love roots deep, though easy loves are legion;
> The heart's as hot and hungry as the hand.
>
> In airless evenings, at the cafe table,
> The soldier sips his thick sweet coffee up:
> The dry grounds, like the moral to my fable,
> Are bitter at the bottom of the cup.

Fraser was important to the Cairo group as an editor and spokesman as well as a contributor. In 'Passages from a Cairo Notebook', he explained how he had organized a literary magazine called *Orientations*. It was started on the premise that such a publication would provide encouragement to the common soldier. 'My idea was to give the common soldier a chance to express himself (outside politics), but the sad fact is that he does not express himself with enough distinction or passion.'[52] The magazine failed but the best poets were successful in continuing to develop their styles and reputations individually. Fraser summed up the poetry of the Cairo group in an article for *Poetry* (*London*) in 1943. 'Cairo's best poems', he wrote, 'will be placid and patient, sad rather than tragic, persuasive rather than minatory, moral rather than prophetic.'[53]

Two of the most underrated poets writing in the Middle East were Bernard Spencer and Terence Tiller. They are important as examples of the spectrum of British poetry written at Cairo. Bernard Spencer, who was published in *New Verse* and was a junior member of the Auden school, is noteworthy (along with Roy Fuller) as a bridge figure from the 1930s to the 1940s. Born in 1909, the same year as Stephen Spender, Spencer was educated at Marlborough and Corpus Christi College, Oxford. He was thirty years old when war was declared. During the war and afterwards, Spencer held British Council posts in Greece, Egypt, Italy, Spain and Turkey. Before he died in Vienna, he produced three volumes of poetry, including one wartime volume: *Aegean Islands* (1946). Spencer's style changed first while he was in Greece where the Mediterranean atmosphere liberated his poetry from the Auden influence. As Roger Bowen has shown, in Spencer we

> witness the transformation of a thirties sensibility made restless by the actuality of war and a role the world at large was still trying to exact from him, and by a slowly evolving awareness that there was a more intense and private self which had been struggling for expression from the beginning.[54]

He moved from what he called a 'rather strangling influence of what was considered right'[55] in the thirties, to the search for 'a dramatic situation in some landscape'. Bowen reminds us that of the fourteen poems which Spencer published in *Personal Landscape*, five of them harboured memories of Greece and the Hellenic world he had been forced to flee. That Grecian landscape never left his memory, just as Fraser could not forget details of his Scottish home town. As Spencer faced the destruction of war, he abandoned his thirties metaphors. He closely observed and bore witness to death, exile, and 'My end of Europe ... at war' ('Salonica, June 1940'). 'Death of an Airman' is fairly representative of his style:

> Dancer's naked foot so earthly planted
> Limbs tall and turned to music of drums; all growth,
> Grass, fountaining palm exulting and vertical,
> Dance his fair hair, his youth.
>
> For when you tread delight as if a wire
> And when your roots in the dark finger earth's springs
> Your strength has an understanding that includes
> Those shot-down wings.

The poem, like most of Spencer's, is not notable for its sentiments or for a complicated texture of thought, but rather for descriptive power. He is best when he is most simple, as in the last two lines. As Bowen notes, his description of soldiers marching in 'Base Town' is also memorable: 'like blood to where a wound is flowing'. But beyond his close observations of war cutting into the landscape, Spencer is interesting for his immersion in the history of the past. 'Sarcophagi', published in *Personal Landscape* in 1942, is one of several striking poems that discover the past as a fragment worth preserving. The past itself is a mausoleum which has strangely survived though buried deep under 'earth's weight' ('Greek Excavations, 1942'). It contains the same social concerns which have always plagued men: 'The minimum wish / For the permanence of the basic things of life, / For children and friends and having enough to eat / And the great key of a skill; / The life the generals and the bankers cheat.'

Spencer also transposed the Hellenic landscape onto Egypt. In 'The Ship', where he dreams of Greece, he previews what will become a major theme, the struggle of dislocation and of finding a subject in his new surroundings:

> No wonder mind should find this scenery bland
> as lotions are to eyes;
> our loves being mostly natives of a land
> mountainous, hung with forests, loud with storms
> and our thoughts climb

to light like things the digger's spade has struck,
a broken dish, a ring,
confused with dark and roots and time.

While Durrell conveyed historical atmosphere more sensuously,
Spencer remained a poet of place and a witness to social events
within landscape. In *Personal Landscape*, volume I, part 4, Spencer
expressed his own views about writing poetry.[56]

> To write good poetry nowadays . . . a poet has to brutalize
> himself back out of his upbringing. His dangers are that, faced
> with injustice, violence and squalor, he may get either numb,
> frigid, over-intellectual, or soft, sentimental. The capacity for
> pity and the capacity for scientific detachment may both be
> valuable to him in the rest of his life but they are dangerous to
> him as a poet. Pity and disgust and the scientific attitude are all
> attitudes of separation, not of joining. True poetry is a dance in
> which you take part and enjoy yourself.

In his poetry Spencer tried to keep a balance. As Roger Bowen has
indicated, Egypt did not stimulate his imagination as much as
Greece did, but it helped trigger the release of other landscapes,
landscapes of home. He explored his separation from England
and his cultural distance from the Middle East. More important,
Spencer's exile continued a process already begun – a growth
towards his own poetic style, one apart from his earlier efforts and
separate from the current London scene.[57]

A very different and more introspective poet, Terence Tiller,
claimed himself as having the representative exile experience. In
The Inward Animal (Cairo, 1942–3), 'framing poems' act as general
statements of alienation, while the central poems describe 'my
own mode of this experience'. For Tiller, exile in an unfamiliar
environment was enough to shake 'a customary self' irrevocably.
His poetry, violently responding to his new surroundings, passed
through three discernible stages: 'rebellion, reconciliation, the
birth of something alien'. Tiller intensely records the 'pain' of
'bearing the child' which is his new self. While many poets just
recorded a threat to identity, Tiller charted an extensive journey
through loss and re-discovery. The 'inward animal' of his title is
that alien self which must be 'so unwillingly conceived and
carried, so harshly brought forth'.

It is clear from Tiller's first collection, *Poems*, published by the Hogarth Press in 1941 and from his wartime poetry volumes, *The Inward Animal* (1943) and *Unarm Eros* (1947), that, like Sidney Keyes and Keith Douglas, he struggles with a passion and a melancholy he wishes to exorcise. In 'Egypt, 1940' Tiller openly accepts the darker side of himself which he associates with the brutality of war. In the first two stanzas below, one senses his peculiar dark night of the soul:

> Now the light finds us; the bright worlds advance
> leaning across Europe's planted lines
> to the uncertain sea
> and the Americas.
> > The night finds us the body betrays us
> > and love devours us and time passes.
>
> This is the hour when carnival is over
> and colours drain from things; the fallacy
> of patient landscapes darkening,
> and man's habitation.
> > The body betrays us and love devours us

While Spencer prefers to describe objects 'stroke by stroke' ('To My Sister'), or to detail some landscape carefully, Tiller confronts a deep inner experience. Tiller and Spencer shared a common locale but developed very different kinds of poetry in their own personal styles. Both aimed for a greater bareness and clarity, and though the results were not always as 'placid' as G. S. Fraser had predicted in *Poetry (London)*, their poetry was intellectually honest and patiently crafted.

V

Among the poets writing during the war, several produced only one or two memorable poems which have been anthologized often because they seem to confront the specific issues of this war: the best-known of these are 'Soldiers Bathing' by F. T. Prince and 'Naming of Parts' by Henry Reed.

F. T. Prince was born in South Africa in 1912 and, after receiving a degree from Oxford and doing postgraduate work at

Princeton, served in the British Intelligence Corps. Although he declared he was not a war poet, 'Soldiers Bathing' was first published in *More Poems from the Forces* edited by Kiedrych Rhys (1946) and was widely reprinted and praised following its discovery by Stephen Spender.

The poem is noteworthy for its triple conjunction of the present moment, the artistic past, and a Christian context. Like the most famous 'religious' poems of the war, *Four Quartets*, 'Soldiers Bathing' grows out of a single actual occurrence into a meditation on art, time, mortality and larger questions of faith. As Prince watches the troops under his rule, he is moved by the vulnerability and weakness of the soldiers:

> The sea at evening moves across the sand.
> Under a reddening sky I watch the freedom of a band
> Of soldiers who belong to me. Stripped bare
> For bathing in the sea, they shout and run in the warm air;
> Their flesh worn by the trade of war, revives
> And my mind towards the meaning of it strives.
>
> All's pathos now. The body that was gross,
> Rank, ravenous, disgusting, in the act or in repose,
> All fever, filth and sweat, its bestial strength
> And bestial decay, by pain and labour grows at length
> Fragile and luminous.

Prince moves in the poem from detachment to re-integration as he views the soldiers, then thinks of two paintings (Michelangelo's cartoon of soldiers bathing and Pollaiuolo's painting of a naked battle), interprets those paintings as a commentary on Christ's crucifixion, and turns back to watching. He sets up three frames of reference: the soldiers' swim, his memory of two paintings, and the archetypal stripping of humanity: Christ's death. In so doing he also achieves a wider and wider cultural significance, as if he were taking a typical romantic lyric and dispossessing the 'I' of its initial fusion with its landscape. However, just as the painting, the art work, is 'indirectly or directly a commentary/ on the Crucifixion' because the 'obverse of the scene', so Christ's death is a commentary on the vision of soldiers' bathing as they rest from the sins He died for. Likewise, the paintings provide commentary on the 'soldiers

who belong to me', for remembering the art works assists the 'I'
towards a fuller comprehension of the pathos he realizes.

The text, then, becomes a circle of reference as one section
re-interprets the others. However, the essence of the poem grows
from the phrase 'war's sorrow and disgrace/ . . . suspended,
stripped' (38–9). Linguistically the phrase is clear in its context;
yet the word *suspension* holds a triple meaning for the poem.
Sorrow 'suspended' refers to the freezing in art of the horrible
brutalities of war. The 'suspension' of war refers to the temporal
possibility of respite from suffering: the soldiers 'stripped bare'
take a swim and relax after fighting all day. This image of war in
all its clarity, as if suspended like a painting, also recalls Christ's
sacrificial death, the body 'suspended' and 'stripped upon the
Cross'. Prince implies the eternal impossibility of any respite from
our sins.

Prince's brilliance in 'Soldiers Bathing' stems from his finally
uniting the three realms he has placed side by side as referents.

> These dry themselves and dress,
> Combing their hair, forget the fear and shame of
>   nakedness.
> Because to love is frightening we prefer
> The freedom of our crimes. Yet, as I drink the
>   dusky air,
> I feel a strange delight that fills me full,
> Strange gratitude, as if evil itself were beautiful,
> And kiss the wound in thought, while in the west
> I watch a streak of red that might have issued from
>   Christ's breast.

Prince's resolution grows from a love that binds him not only to
his men but also to that 'great love' which 'has driven us to this
fury'. From a detachment through memory and speculation, he
returns to *These* soldiers bathing. He is re-integrated into the scene
before him, and though he has reinterpreted the 'freedom of a
band of soldiers' in light of the 'freedom of our crimes' he does not
despair. He 'sees' that though man is a fallen Adam and a Cain, he
is part of a larger union of worlds and temporal realms where
opposites like evil and good or filth and purity are more nearly
indistinguishable.

Henry Reed, like Prince, had written only one volume of poetry when war ended. He was born in Birmingham in 1914 and worked as a freelance journalist before war broke out. Though his participation in the army was brief, his series of poems 'The Lessons of War' (from *A Map of Verona*, 1946) are among the best known poems of the Second World War. 'Naming of Parts' is the first poem in this series. Like 'Soldiers Bathing', 'Naming of Parts' is a meditative poem; however, its central conflict concerns a separation between a recruit's wandering thoughts and an army officer's voice of instruction. Reed counterpoints the language of Basic Training to lyrical phrases describing 'the neighbour gardens'.

> Today we have naming of parts. Yesterday
> We had daily cleaning. And tomorrow morning,
> We shall have what to do after firing. But today,
> Today we have naming of parts. Japonica
> Glistens like coral in all of the neighbour gardens
>   And today we have naming of parts.

Just as the poem contrasts two worlds – the mechanical army training session and the lush world of nature – it also juxtaposes two selves, that of officer and that of recruit. While the officer drones on from memory, the recruit allies himself with the active beauty and sexuality of nature, with the bees pollinating 'backwards and forwards'.

If the sexual dimension of the officer's language is lost on the recruit, it is certainly not lost on the reader who is consistently made aware of the phallic weapon of war and the gardens it will penetrate. The irony of 'not having': 'And this is the piling swivel, / Which in your case you have not got'; 'and the point of balance / Which in our case we have not got,' is part of a more serious statement. For in this lesson about a phallic weapon, a part is missing. The gun, and the war it represents – the diminished, endless, boring, hierarchical, stupid war – are set in contrast to the recruit's sensual imagination, keen to physical beauty: the japonica glistens, 'The blossoms are fragile and motionless', 'the almond-blossom silent'. Though phallic, war is also impotent in comparison to man's own private lusts. Reed views the war as inhuman and degrading; in contrast, his recruit's potency is the glory which the poem's epigraph mentions: 'Vixi duellis nuper idoneus / Et militavi non sine gloria'.

Both Prince and Reed exalt the distinctly human in their highly meditative war poems. The speakers are soldiers, yet the most important feelings in Reed's poem are not spoken, as though the private man has no voice worth hearing compared with man-as-soldier. The poets of this war, whether at home, abroad, in service, or civilians, find meaning in cameo-narratives of individual experience.

NOTES

1. Stephen Spender, 'War Poetry in this War', *The Listener*, 16 (16 October 1941) p. 539.
2. 'To the Poets of 1940', *TLS* (30 December 1940) p. 755.
3. See Jon Silkin, *Out of Battle, The Poetry of the Great War* (Oxford: Oxford University Press, 1972) p. 202; Paul Fussell, *The Great War and Modern Memory* (New York: Oxford University Press, 1975) pp. 75–112. Also see his further remarks on the two wars as a single historical episode, pp. 317–18.
4. Spender, 'War Poetry in this War'.
5. See Jon Silkin (ed.), *The Penguin Book of First World War Poetry* (Harmondsworth: Penguin, 1979) Introduction. Also see: Robert Wohl, *The Generation of 1914* (Cambridge: Harvard University Press, 1979) Chapter 2.
6. Personal interviews with G. S. Fraser, 6 November 1979 and Peter Porter, 16 November 1979. Also see John Guenther, *Sidney Keyes* (London: London Magazine Editions, 1967) p. 219.
7. Spender, 'War Poetry in this War'.
8. H. B. Mallalieu, 'Some Autobiographical Statements' in Ian Hamilton, (ed.), *The Poetry of War 1939–45* (London: Alan Ross, 1965) p. 167.
9. Robert Graves, 'War Poetry in this War', *The Listener*, 26 (23 October 1941) p. 566.
10. Clifford Dyment, *Time and Tide* (2 January 1943) as quoted by Robert Hewison, *Under Siege* (London: Weidenfeld & Nicolson, 1977) p. 118.
11. Ronald Blythe, *Components of the Scene*, an anthology (Harmondsworth: Penguin, 1966) Introduction.
12. Gavin Ewart, as quoted in Oscar Williams, *The War Poets* (New York: Day and Co.) pp. 28–9.
13. Keith Douglas, letter to J. C. Hall, 10 August 1943. Add. Ms. 56355 British Library. Also quoted in A. Banerjee, *Spirit Above Wars* (London: Macmillan of India, 1976) p. 122.
14. Mildred Davidson, *The Poetry is in the Pity* (New York: Barnes and Noble, 1972) p. 96.
15. Alun Lewis, *Letters from India* (Cardiff: Penmark Press, 1946) p. 49.
16. Personal interview with John Heath-Stubbs, 8 November 1979.
17. Personal interview with John Lehmann, 3 July 1980.
18. John Lehmann and John Heath-Stubbs in interviews.
19. Angus Calder, *The People's War, Britain 1939–1945* (New York: Pantheon Books, 1969) pp. 475–6.
20. Philip Larkin, *Jill* (New York: The Woodstock Press, 1976), p. 9. Also see

Richard Hillary's memories in *The Last Enemy* (London: Macmillan, 1942) pp. 10, 13, 28.

21. Elizabeth Bowen, *The Heat of the Day* (New York: Knopf, 1949) p. 46.
22. Michael Howard, 'The 1940s', *The Cherwell* (11 November 1970) p. 7.
23. Roland Loewe, 'Wartime Letter', in Donald Bain (ed.), *Oxford and Cambridge Writing* (Cambridge: Cambridge University Press, 1942) p. 8.
24. John Waller, 'Massacre in the High', *The Cherwell* (21 January 1939) pp. 6–8.
25. Stephen Spender, 'The Influence of Rilke on English Poetry', *The Listener* 36 (18 July 1946) p. 84. Also see: Sidney Keyes, letter to John Heath-Stubbs, 20 February 1943, as quoted by Michael Meyer in *The Collected Poems of Sidney Keyes* (London: George Routledge, 1945) pp. xviii–xxi. Also see Alun Lewis' poem 'To Rilke', in Ian Hamilton (ed.), *Selected Poetry and Prose* (London: George Allen & Unwin, 1966) pp. 105–6.
26. Rilke, quoted by Spender in 'The Influence of Rilke on English Poetry'.
27. Philip Larkin, letter to the author, 25 July 1980.
28. John Heath-Stubbs, interview with G. H. B. Wightman in *Aquarius*, The John Heath-Stubbs Issue, 10 (1978) p. 81.
29. Philip Larkin, *The North Ship* (London: Faber & Faber, 1966 edn) pp. 8–9.
30. Larkin, *The North Ship*.
31. Keith Douglas, in Keith Douglas and Alec M. Hardie (eds), *Augury* (Oxford: Basil Blackwell, 1940) p. xiv.
32. See Desmond Graham, *Keith Douglas, 1920–1944, A Biography* (London: Oxford University Press, 1974) pp. 85–6.
33. Larkin, *The North Ship*.
34. Michael Meyer, 'The 1940s', *The Cherwell* (11 November 1970) p. 12.
35. Michael Meyer, 'John Heath-Stubbs in the Forties', in Dannie Abse (ed.), *Best Poetry of the Year 6* (London: Robson Books, 1979) p. 181.
36. Sidney Keyes, Introduction to Sidney Keyes and Michael Meyer (eds), *Eight Oxford Poets* (London: George Routledge, 1941) p. vii.
37. Keith Douglas, letter to Margaret Stanley-Wrench, 1941, Add. Ms. 57977 British Library.
38. Michael Sharp (ed.), *The Poems of Drummond Allison* (Reading: White Knights Press, 1978, limited edition) p. xv.
39. Hewison, *Under Siege*, p. 124.
40. Keyes, *Eight Oxford Poets*, p. viii.
41. Peter Ratazzi, *Khaki and Blue*, Armed Forces magazine (Summer 1944) p. 57.
42. Douglas Grant, 'War and the Writer', *Penguin Parade* II, 3 (1957).
43. Gavin Ewart, 'Autobiographical Statements', in *The Poetry of War 1939–45*, p. 164.
44. Roy Fuller, 'Autobiographical Statements', in *The Poetry of War 1939–45*, p. 165.
45. Personal interview with Roy Fuller, 22 November 1979. Also see Fuller's revised war poems from 'an old file', two of which, 'The First Winter of War' and 'Embarkation in Wartime', are published in *The Listener* 82 (4 December 1969) pp. 798–9 and the other seven which are published in *An Old War* (Edinburgh: The Tragara Press, 1974, limited edition). And see John Lehmann, *Thrown to the Woolfs* (London: Weidenfeld & Nicolson, 1978) pp. 119–22.

46. Robin Fedden (ed.), *Personal Landscape, An Anthology of Exile* (London: Editions Poetry London, 1945), p. 7.
47. Ibid., p. 8.
48. Olivia Manning, 'Poets in Exile', *Horizon* (October, 1944) p. 270.
49. Ibid., p. 273.
50. Fedden, *Personal Landscape*, p. 9.
51. Personal interview with G. S. Fraser, 6 November 1979.
52. G. S. Fraser, 'Passages from a Cairo Notebook', *Leaves from the Storm*, p. 163.
53. G. S. Fraser, 'Recent Verse: London and Cairo', *Poetry (London)*, volume 2, X (1944) p. 217.
54. Roger Bowen, 'Native and Exile: The Poetry of Bernard Spencer', *Malahat Review* (January, 1979) pp. 6–7.
55. Bernard Spencer, interview with Peter Orr, *The Poet Speaks* (London: Routledge & Kegan Paul, 1966) p. 234.
56. Bernard Spencer, 'Ideas About Poems', *Personal Landscape*, vol. I, pt. 4.
57. For detailed descriptions of London poetry during the war, especially the 'society' of Fitzrovia, see Hewison, *Under Siege*, note 10; Derek Stanford, *Inside the Forties* (London: Sidgwick & Jackson, 1977); Dan Davin, *Closing Times* (London: Oxford University Press, 1975); and Michell Raper, 'Fitzrovia and the War', *The Listener* (3 October 1974) pp. 428–9.

4　Two Poets of War: Alun Lewis and Sidney Keyes

Of the many service poets in the Second World War, three stand above the rest:[1] Alun Lewis (1915–44), Sidney Keyes (1922–43) and Keith Douglas (1920–44). While Douglas, who willingly gave himself over to war, merits separate consideration, Lewis and Keyes provide a striking contrast in their literary responses to the realities of a war they did not wish to join. Lewis writes as an intelligent average man; lonely and bored, he resents war as a hindrance to his artistic development. Older than Keyes, Lewis had already started writing poetry in a style that was no longer suitable to capture the traumas of worldwide holocaust. His achievement during war-time illustrates a poet caught between two social worlds, two styles, and two modes of commitment: pacifism and activism. The more romantic and esoteric Keyes transferred to landscapes of war the subjective battles he had metaphorically represented earlier. His poetry also reflects the metaphysical strain to be found in wartime writing – a search for structures of belief in time of unrelenting chaos. Both men wrote elegiac poetry to express an acute sense of displacement. Each also came to accept the death he eventually met.

When thinking of Lewis and Keyes it is helpful to recall one of the major mythic leit-motivs that plays throughout Second World War literature, the drowned man. According to epic tradition, the drowned sailor, like Palinurus in the *Aeneid*, was not a hero but a steersman who fell asleep at the helm of the hero's ship, or at his watchpoint, and tumbled to death. The drowned man is, of course, a type who reappeared with variations throughout literature, from Elpenor in the *Odyssey*, to Cowper's Castaway, to Phlebas the Phoenician of *The Waste Land* to Cyril Connolly's appropriated Palinurus in *The Unquiet Grave* (1945). Though not an Aeneas or an Odysseus figure, the sailor represents that part of the hero with control over his own destiny. When he dies, the hero must go on alone into the depths of the underworld – fated, he has no human control over his boat/his life. Carl Jung, who gained a wide reputation in the 1930s partly through the studies of Maud Bodkin and others interested in literary archetypes, believed that man must take such a drowning voyage in order to be reborn into a better self. Like the drowned sailor with whom Keyes openly identified, he and Lewis were completely overwhelmed by historical events. They viewed themselves as victims of circumstances that they could only struggle to understand.

Unlike poets of the First World War, Lewis and Keyes did not write propaganda poetry. In addition, neither of them actually saw as much direct action as Owen or Sassoon had seen in the First World War, or Douglas would see in the Second World War. They rarely showed the battlefield's death masks to those at home. Nor did they bring to army life idealistic preconceptions in need of readjustment or shattering. Rather, they brought the personal problems of belief which they had begun to explore in time of peace – questions of commitment, ambivalences about violence, fears of death by technological society. Alun Lewis' poetry and prose record his frustrations in responding to the external events of war. Keyes turned inward and wrote essentially intimate psychological documents. In raising personal questions against the panorama of war, they both asserted the spirit of individuality in a war which, more than any other, denied the individual identity.

I   ALUN LEWIS

> 'But I've got a persistent feeling that I'm still waiting for my big moment, my big word.'
>
> 6 December 1943[2]

In a journal entry describing a dream-meeting with Rainer Maria Rilke, the twenty-seven-year-old Alun Lewis, soon to land on the Indian sub-continent and fated to die fourteen months later, recalled that Robert Graves had written: 'Milton would have profited from serving in the army'. Lewis demurred. 'But I don't know whether this is so, some men have – it seems to destroy others.'[3] This thoughtful scepticism, which borders on indecisiveness and deflects from the visionary nature of his dream-meeting, seems characteristic of Lewis. War may have helped sharpen or enlarge the work of some poets: Roy Fuller discovered new themes and landscapes; for Sidney Keyes, war presented the death he earlier had only been able to court imaginatively, and Keith Douglas found war to be a necessary and logical stage in his programmatic development as a poet. For Alun Lewis, however, it only accentuated an indecisiveness he felt could not be resolved until the war was over.

'Acceptance seems so spiritless', Lewis wrote from India to his wife Gweno, 'protest so vain. In between the two I live.'[4] Ian Hamilton rightly calls Lewis a 'divided man', but also proposes that Lewis' life involved a key struggle between his active and contemplative sides.[5] Instead, Lewis better fits Matthew Arnold's description of the indecisive wanderer who remains lost between two worlds. The strains of army life in England and abroad deprived Lewis of a secure solitude he badly needed in order to create. Turning away from a long autobiographical prose work he had been planning, Lewis was forced to cling to shorter art forms. As early as the autumn of 1939, he had complained, 'Ach! What was the good of writing a long novel when I couldn't see the way into the next day'.[6] Far from embracing war, Lewis felt it as an interruption which would eventually end. Unlike Sidney Keyes and Keith Douglas, who managed to fashion imaginative battlefields, he sought a peacefulness and love left behind in Wales. Yet even that solace is questioned by his doubting mind.

Throughout his prose and poetry, Lewis consistently wavers in his commitment to the present war. In one of his last literary productions, a short story called 'Ward "0" 3 (b)'[7] Lewis still finds himself reconsidering his relationship to the past and his reasons for enlisting. The story concerns four wounded soldiers awaiting medical board decisions in a British General Hospital in India in 1943. Of these four soldiers, Anthony Weston is a self-portrait of Lewis. In an important conversation with another patient, Brownlow-Grace, Weston stresses not only the social divisions between them but his own self-division:

'Look,' says Weston, 'I didn't start with the same things as you. You had a pram and a private school and you saw the sea, maybe. My father was a collier and he worked in a wet pit. He got rheumatism and nystagmus and then the dole and then parish relief. I'm not telling you a sob story. It's just I was used

to different sounds. I used to watch the wheel of the pit spin
round year after year, after school and Saturdays and Sundays;
and then from 1926 on I watched it not turning round at all, and
I can't never get that wheel out of my mind. It spins and idles
. . . Against that wheel in my head, I didn't get on very well.

Weston's first impulse was to get away from the wheel of the past
which would suck him under, yet in his desire to escape, he
wandered aimlessly towards an unnamed goal. Having landed a
job in a Holborn book shop, he became fascinated by one of his
regular customers, a Frenchwoman.

I asked this chap about her. He said she was a big name, you
know the way revolutionary movements toss up a woman
sometimes. She was a Communist, a big speaker in the
industrial towns in North France, she's been to Russia too.
And, well, I just wanted her, more and more and more as the
months passed. Not her politics, but her fire. If I could hear her
addressing a crowd, never mind about wanting her in those
dreams you get.

At first, Weston compares his lust for political affiliation to his
desire for a woman, yet when he meets a committed Communist,
he seems to identify her with something other than particular
ideologies. The woman represents a direction and fire which the
artist manqué needs, but cannot name. He follows her as if she
were a Muse and has an affair with her in France, an affair from
which he never recovers. He takes her spirit to the battlefield as
his reason for fighting: 'The whole fortnight after we made that
last stand with Martel at Cambrai I didn't know whether I was
looking for her or Dunkirk'. Weston's impulse towards politics is
revealed to be an involvement for its own sake. Still suffering from
her farewell letter, Weston turns to Brownlow-Grace for comfort,
but he is rebuffed. Brownlow-Grace goes off to spend the evening
with a woman of his own, and Weston is left behind. Feeling
doubly isolated, he turns to one of the other men, Moncrieff, a
projection of his own helpless loneliness and passivity. Moncrieff
(even the name sounds like 'my grief') is a cripple who wants
desperately to go home but must stay in India until the authorities
decide his fate. Governed by others, he remains a passive victim.
Throughout the story, Weston describes himself as a 'ready'

fighter – a struggling rebel in his battle with a mining wheel, a passionate student of politics, an ardent lover; yet as Alun Lewis seems to realize in his characterization of Weston, this wounded soldier has never truly left his past nor has he even been able to commit himself to a present. He remains unable to act, and only when history acts upon him does he decide to go to war. Tranquillity suits him far better than the fire he thought he wanted – like Moncrieff, he has been crippled. ' "I like the pool," Moncrieff said. They strolled out together and sat on the circular ledge. The curving bright branches held their leaves peacefully above the water.' Weston responds to the flowing nature of the water even as his own nature is an oscillating one: 'And as they [the waves] lapped inwards he felt the ripples surging against the most withdrawn and inmost ledges of his being, like a series of temptations in the wilderness. And he felt glad.' He takes refuge in an ignorant happiness, unwilling to face his own reflection in Moncrieff's 'empty inarticulate eyes'.

Weston is not, of course, an exact replica of Lewis, but the events of his life and his hesitant and peace-seeking nature bears a strong resemblance to those of the Welsh poet. The eldest of four children, Alun Lewis was born on 1 July 1915 in Aberdare, South Wales, the son of a schoolmaster. Reared in the mining district, he would not forget the poverty of his homeland or the industrializa-tion which destroyed a Welsh pastoral beauty. At seventeen Lewis sat the entrance examinations for Jesus College, Oxford, but the examiners considered him too young and advised him to reapply. He chose a scholarship to Aberystwyth rather than a deferred entrance to Oxford. At university he took an easy First in History but puzzled over a career. His professor R. F. Traherne described Lewis' choice as between 'the ideal of a writer's life, to be attained by way of journalism', or a career of 'research and teaching'.[8] Lewis chose research and proceeded to Manchester University where he obtained an MA in Medieval History, but he was unhappy with his decision. Still unsure of the best course of action, he completed a teacher's training course and found a job at Pengam.

As the threat of war became the common cause, Lewis struggled openly between activism and pacifism. In a letter to Richard Mills in May 1939 he spoke of the 'army, the bloody, silly, ridiculous red-faced army – in its boring khaki – God save me from joining up'.[9] In August his tone was different: 'I shall probably join up, I imagine. I've been unable to settle the moral issue satisfactorily'. Lewis knew that the war was necessary, that fascism must be stopped, but he could see no reason for killing. In the same letter, Lewis maintained that he was a writer first and a moralist second, but above all a man desirous of experiencing life in as many phases as possible. By 1940, when he was due for conscription, he had met the woman he would marry, Gweno Ellis. His plan to join her brothers in the Merchant Navy aboard the *S.S. Anglo-Saxon* was a near certainty. But at the last moment, as Ian Hamilton notes, he changed his mind, and unable to explain why later on, he joined the Army.

Lewis' ideological commitments, then, altered dramatically from the late thirties when he was a pacifist, to 1944 when he died on duty in Burma. He flirted with becoming a conscientious objector before volunteering for a non-combative unit in the Royal Engineers. Commissioned as an officer in the Infantry, he was posted to India in 1943. The circumstances of his death remain mysterious. It is reported that while he patrolled in the Maya Hills (he had chosen to stay in combat instead of leaving his men), he slipped on a rocky path and fell, mortally wounded by his loaded revolver. He died on 5 March 1944.

Just before he went to India, Lewis pondered his double role as artist and soldier. A short story entitled 'Dusty Hermitage', written at this point, significantly explores his profound ambivalences toward personal and public commitment. Once again Lewis appears in the guise of a sensitive soldier. The soldier, about to go off to war, pays a call on the memory of the last romantic war hero. He visits the National Trust cottage of T. E. Lawrence, lovingly looked after by a girl who knew Lawrence well. Like Lawrence, the soldier drives a motorbike and appears to the girl as 'another such as he'.

Lewis' soldier is both drawn to Lawrence and yet indifferent to him; his ambivalence is represented by the other characters in the story who choose one attitude or the other towards the dead hero. For example, the girl caretaker represents a devotion and commitment which the soldier would like to match, yet cannot. Her ties to Lawrence are emphasized in the opening lines: 'She had had the key of his cottage ever since his death, and at least once a week she had gone in and dusted it, opened the window, put fresh flowers in the music room, and run the brown water out of the taps'. At the opposite extreme are two visitors to the cottage, a married couple, who represent an unimaginative and uncaring lack of identification with this dead man and his simple life. They are symbolic of the conforming capitalist mentality that makes Lawrence into a 'great man', reads the *Daily Mirror* and asks questions about indoor lavatories and financial resources. In contrast, the soldier possesses 'wide perceptive eyes that were more contemplative and sensitive than inquisitive'. In a conversation with the girl, he dwells on Lawrence as an artist:

> 'He was an artist,' the soldier said slowly . . . 'but an artist who couldn't commit himself to his choice.' 'How do you mean?' she asked. 'Well, the artist has the best chance of pursuing the good,' he said, 'because as an artist he had no vested interests in the warring elements. He is just so much an artist as he is disinterested. But that is only his potential. His actual power depends on the vigour with which he pursues his choice once he has made it. He couldn't make a positive choice. That's why he was unfulfilled.'

The young woman, herself unfulfilled and yet someone who has made a positive choice, turns the tables on her visitor: ' "You have chosen?" she said, smiling a trifle ironically.' But when the soldier attempts a half-completed answer 'evading her without being evasive', she recognizes his further kinship to Lawrence: 'that was a habit she had met before also'. Here as in 'Ward "0" 3 (b)' the woman represents some sort of conscience which the artist needs and values. As in his poetry, Lewis understands the need for commitment. But just as the soldier contritely apologizes for 'poking his nose' into another man's house, so does Lewis waver here. He divides himself into the dutiful and loving woman, the indifferent couple, and the hesitant soldier-narrator. Only a half-entertained death-wish can resolve the story's conflicts: Lewis stresses the soldier's 'suddenly carefree' attitude as he drives off on his motorbike along the same road (and on the same day at almost the same hour) on which T. E. Lawrence had 'swerved' to meet his fatal accident.

In creating a protagonist who is more sensitive than inquisitive, Lewis seems to acknowledge that the Arnoldian disinterestedness he covets eludes him as much as it eludes the young soldier. But his story carries a double irony. While Lewis seems to shirk identification with T. E. Lawrence, he also recognizes an undeniable resemblance. Samuel Hynes' description of Lawrence as one who 'made himself into a man of action as though by an act of will and then withdrew again'[10] seems to fit Lewis quite well. In spite of Alun John's warning that Lewis' personal life is less important than his poems,[11] the ambivalent lack of focus or shifts in style are directly connected to his temperament and the milieu of war. War thus made Lewis into a poet, but it also claimed him as a victim.

Had the war not intervened, Lewis might well have become a regional novelist. Even during the war his goal was to return to Wales and write of the mining villages, a heritage he knew and about which he felt passionately. During the war years 1939–44 he wrote ninety-five poems and twenty-six stories,[12] which were collected in four volumes: *Raiders' Dawn* (1942), *The Last Inspection* (stories, 1942), *Ha! Ha! Among the Trumpets* (1943); the posthumous *Letters from India* and *In the Green Tree* (stories) were published in 1946 and 1948.

Lewis' poetry reflects an inner ambiguity heightened by war and often seems to work against itself, either by mixing styles or mismatching style and subject. In a poem like 'The Soldier', for instance (where he may be recalling Rupert Brooke), Lewis tries to confront experience directly but is deflected into an hysterical tone which then subsides into an easily achieved calm. The following two stanzas are representative.

> I within me holding
> Turbulence and time
> – Volcanic fires deep beneath the glacier –
> Feel the dark cancer in my vitals
> Of impotent impatience grope its way
> Through daze and dream to throat and fingers
> To find its climax of disaster.
>
>   . . . .
>   Yet still
> I who am agonized by thought
> And war and love
> Grow calm again
> With watching
> The flash and play of finches
> Who are as beautiful
> And indifferent to me
> As England is, this Spring morning.

As the soldier in 'Dusty Hermitage' peers into another man's life but apologizes for it, so here Lewis engages his own mental conflicts but retreats. The poem expresses the utter impossibility of welding two different worlds that society itself has sundered through political events. In his fiction he is able to divide responses over a larger canvas into different characters; in the short lyric he is pushed to a compression where conflicting impulses lock in a headlong battle.[13] Often unable to integrate warring realms, Lewis' poetry conveys well that strong sense of personal disintegration, loss and alienation felt by so many during the forties.

In his love poems, such as 'Postscript: for Gweno', while there is a slight jarring of tones, he masters a conflict between opposed worlds by giving allegiance to a love that can withstand even the horrors of death itself:

> If I should go away,
> Beloved, do not say
> 'He has forgotten me.'
> For you abide,
> A singing rib within my dreaming side;
> You always stay.
> And in the mad tormented valley
> Where blood and hunger rally
> And Death the wild beast is uncaught, untamed,
> Our soul withstands the terror
> And has its quiet honour
> Among the glittering stars your voices named.

Yet some of Lewis' best poetry grows directly from his prose-writer's understanding of the power of concrete detail. In 'After Dunkirk', Lewis turns aside from self-pity to a vivid projection of anger at others. Opening on a confessional note stressing silence and tears, the poem seems to search for its subject:

> I have been silent a lifetime
> As a stabbed man,
> And stolid showing nothing
> As a refugee
> But inwardly I have wept.

Lewis learns 'to speak again', and his poem immediately comes
alive as soon as he turns to what he has perceived in the world
around him, the barracks life:

> The subterfuges of democracy, the stench
> Of breath in crowded tents, the grousing queues,
> And bawdy songs incessantly resung
> And dull relaxing in the dirty bar;
> The difficult tolerance of all that is
> Mere rigid brute routine.

The writer who had hoped to depict the realism of Welsh mining
towns succeeded best when dealing with solid images and objects.
Likewise, the egalitarian who opposed industrialization, the
democratic simple man, 'fired' his poetry in an explosion of anger
at class divisions, the boredom and lack of integrity of army life.
Just as Arnold has laid aside his sense of loss when battling other
critics with zest and wit, so Lewis sidestepped the whole question
of commitment when he fiercely assaulted the Philistinism of the
1940s. In poems such as 'The Sentry' and 'Infantry', he recorded
his distress and anger at 'the reality of war' which came like 'a jab
in the stomach',[14] and the nasty experience of being an officer.[15]
His account of the routine soldier's life in these poems also
provided the backbone for some of his best short stories, stories
such as 'Lance Jack'[16] where he wrote:

> In the army you begin again. All you were seems to have
> vanished. It was simply another mode of life, Civvy Street. I
> was a school teacher in a big secondary school, a responsible
> and exacting job. Now I clean latrines, windows, barrack-
> rooms, run errands for snooty little office clerks with stripes on
> their arms, listen to filthy talk shouted from bed to bed, suffer a
> series of violent reactions.

Nowhere did Lewis succeed better in poetry or prose than in
'All Day It Has Rained', probably his most famous poem. As soon
as it appeared in *Horizon* in January 1941, Robert Graves hailed
Lewis as the War Poet the nation had been waiting for. It began
his reputation and earned him his first book contract with Allen
and Unwin for *Raiders' Dawn*, a volume which inluded the poem.
In 'All Day It Has Rained', Lewis recreates the dream-like

quality of wartime waiting. Soldiers smoke, darn socks, read the
Sunday papers, talk of women, imagine their next military
offensive; yet they remain indifferent, even neutral to their
experiences. They are numb to feeling in the grey haze of mist and
rain. And here, perhaps because of the inspiration of Edward
Thomas, who stands behind this poem, Lewis is able for once to
combine realism with naturalism and nostalgia. He places
ephemeral man in the permanent setting of mist and achieves an
integration of worlds.

> All day it has rained, and we on the edge of the moors
> Have sprawled in our bell-tents, moody and dull as boors,
> Ground sheets and blankets spread on the muddy ground
> And from the first grey wakening we have found
> No refuge from the skirmish
> And the wind that made the canvas heave and flap
> And the taut wet guy-ropes ravel out and snap.
>
> . . .
>
> And we talked of girls, and dropping bombs on Rome,
> And thought of the quiet dead and the loud celebrities
> Exhorting us to slaughter, and the herded refugees;
> – Yet thought softly, morosely of them, and as indifferently
> As of ourselves or those whom we
> For years have loved, and will again
> Tomorrow maybe love; but now it is the rain
> Possesses us entirely, the twilight and the rain.

This mist prompts memories of home:

> And I can remember nothing dearer or more to my heart
> Than the children I watched in the woods on Saturday
> Shaking down burning chestnuts for the schoolyard's merry
>   play,
> Or the shaggy patient dog who followed me
> By sheet and steep and up the wooded scree
> To the Shoulder o'Mutton where Edward Thomas brooded
>   long
> On death and beauty – till a bullet stopped his song.

The final brutal line jolts the reader. Alluring as the recollections
of domesticity and the past may be, there can be no escape into

dreams from the realities of war and death. The snap of the
guy-ropes is echoed by a bullet crack which sunders the integration of man and the natural world.

Throughout his life, Lewis recognized a 'goal' which remained
mysterious and vague. Sometimes he sought his goal in action
personified by war service, sometimes in a silent peace allied to
death. He seems to have weighed each alternative again with
equal care as he embarked for India. He urged his wife to leave her
teaching job and volunteer for the Red Cross: 'I say we must lose
ourselves in the war and go each into the unknown and neither of
us must cling to a past memory or a future hope but we must give
to the world and suffer the world become its accidents [*sic*], and so
grow rich'.[17] In a poem Lewis began on the second day of his
voyage to India he calls again on Gweno 'NOT to withdraw into
the hard core of waiting and lacking', but to project herself – 'to all
waking and surprising sights, all sadness and realities, all
cruelties':

> For you who feared not love fear not to go
> Where bitter knives give blow on counter blow.[18]

Both of these messages to Gweno also call to half of Lewis, that
half which identified so strongly with the women of commitment
in his stories. As he went to India, part of him yearned for action,
and he took pleasure in working for his men. Accepting a job of
entertainment officer aboard ship, he felt that at last he was doing
something constructive.

But Lewis could never rest with such a quasi-commitment, for
he also needed an isolation free from responsibilities. In 'To
Rilke', begun on the ship and concluded on shore, Lewis describes
a moment when he attained the impersonal silence he sought:

> The sea is gone now and the crowded tramp
> Sails other seas with other passengers.
> I sit within the tent, within the darkness
> Of India, and the wind disturbs my lamp.
>
> The jackals howl and whimper in the nullah,
> The goatherd sleeps upon a straw-piled bed,
> And I know that in this it does not matter
> Where one may be or what fate lies ahead.

And Vishnu, carved by some rude pious hand,
Lies by a heap of stones, demanding nothing
But the simplicity that she and I
Discovered in a way you'd understand
Once and forever, Rilke, but in Oh a distant land.

The *she* in this poem, Gweno in England, represents a unification of spirit linked with simplicity and acceptance – and with Rilke. Rilke seems to possess such a union and thus to hold out possibilities which Lewis despairs of attaining. Though 'To Rilke' celebrates such an attainment, it also questions the poet's ability to preserve the simplicity he has discovered but lost. John Lehmann has compared Lewis with Wordsworth for his love of nature and the human heart,[19] but he is certainly un-Wordsworthian in his self-distrust. He gravely doubts his ability to revivify and repossess an experience in tranquillity. In fact, this poem stresses his distance from the great visionaries such as Rilke and Wordsworth: labour, exile, and fatigue hinder Lewis.

In his poems of 1943 and 1944, death becomes the only realm where such integration is really possible. 'Shadows' expresses his choice of a state beyond time:

He chooses best who does not choose
Time and all its lies;
Who makes the end and the beginning One
Within himself, grows wise.

Here Lewis proposes that an acceptance of limitation brings peace. He appears to choose, yet even in his commitment to this neutral zone he avoids taking a side. He commits himself to an unidentifiable abstraction: 'a One'.

It is in poems like 'Burma Casualty', however, that the lure of death acquires a new intensity. The wounded soldier thinks of dead comrades whom 'the dark enfolds / So secretly'. Asking himself why his friends had stayed behind, 'he knew':

The dark is a beautiful singing sexless angel
Her hands so soft you scarcely feel her touch
Gentle, eternally gentle, round your heart.
She flatters and unsexes every man.

Life, on the other hand, is here equated with a demanding, ugly and unkempt masculine figure, a 'crude, pigheaded churl / Frowsy and starving, daring to suffer alone'. Lewis embraces death as preferable to life, as he may well have done in his mysterious pistol 'accident', overcome finally, perhaps, by the same allurement of the 'unsexing' heart of darkness.

'The Jungle' represents one last attempt to resolve ambivalences toward the 'warring demands' of life. At first the jungle is described as lovely. Yet its beauty fearfully suffocates and isolates, much like the loveliness of the island that dehumanizes Tennyson's Lotos-Eaters or the Circean magic which reduces Odysseus' men to swine. 'In mole-blue indolence the sun / Plays idly on the stagnant pool / In whose grey bed black swollen leaf / Holds Autumn rotting like an unfrocked priest.' It is a world where all 'strength of mind and limb must pass / And all fidelities and doubts dissolve'.

Formerly, as in 'Dusty Hermitage', 'Ward "0" 3 (b)', and 'To Rilke', Lewis longed for a commitment personified by the opposite sex. If only he could attain and internalize it, a division would heal. But the fact that he now seems to focus on a stone statue or a neuter jungle shows his ever deeper alienation from life and a certain acknowledgement of failure.

Lewis' voyage into the unknown regions of his personality failed to yield a philosophy or a resolution. 'The Jungle' only intensifies the alienation he had earlier tried to combat in poems such as 'Postscript: for Gweno'. In the cold and noisy scene around him, he is moved to question death itself:

> The bamboos creak like an uneasy house;
> The night is shrill with crickets, cold with space.
> And if the mute pads on the sand should lift
> Annihilating paws and strike us down
> Then would some unimportant death resound
> With the imprisoned music of the soul?
> And we become the world we could not change?
> Or does the will's long struggle end
> With the last kindness of a foe or friend?

In his last poem, Lewis thus remains characteristically sceptical. Death may come as the kind act of another man, and not as the result of cruel aggression against the enemy. Death then, can become something received and passively accepted for itself. There is a pacifist's as well as a warrior's death. And death paradoxically removes conflict and relieves alienation, taking man from the arms of the killer into its own sexless embrace.

II SIDNEY KEYES

'I would like to reject the whole outer world, even to destroy it; another time I feel something resembling physical desire for it.'
(Letter to Milein Cosmann, 21 June 1942)

Unlike Alun Lewis, Sidney Keyes found in war the needed objective correlatives for his own inner turmoil. In that sense, he was a war poet from the very start, and not, as Hewison has maintained, 'simply someone killed while in the services',[20] because his experiences at the Front lasted for a bare two weeks. Not only did his early death cut short a career of promise, but it also robbed him of an opportunity to refine and deepen the exploration of his central themes: death, pain and separation.

Although Keyes died at an even younger age than Lewis (he was only twenty-one), life had dealt harshly with him from the beginning. Born in Dartford, Kent in 1922, he was an only child whose mother died shortly after his birth. His father Reginald, attempting to refashion his personal life, entrusted Sidney to the care of his own parents who lived nearby.

Painfully broken relationships seem to have dominated three generations of the Keyes family. Sidney's grandfather, Sidney Killworth Keyes, married three times; Sidney's father, too, married three times (Sidney Keyes was the child of his second wife). And Sidney's own love relationships were not simple ones. A sickly child, he was kept out of school in charge of a locally-hired nurse until he was nine years old. Occasionally his father visited, but by and large, Reginald took little interest in the child. Other family members also remained distant. The resulting isolation and alienation forced Sidney to turn within to a world of fantasy, literary heroes, and mythic conceptions of those around him. On the natural world of Kent, he superimposed the heroic and macabre world of his own imagination. When Sidney was nine, his grandfather remarried and his new wife removed the child to Dartford Grammar School where he studied for three years before taking entrance exams to Tonbridge School, his father's *alma mater*.

It is not surprising that Keyes' first poem should have been a lament. 'Elegy', written when he was sixteen, is a memorial to his grandfather. Its sophistication and assured voice immediately signal a strong poetic talent.

A key to many later poems, 'Elegy' represents much more than a youthful interest in death by a poet who would deliberately dub himself 'romantic'.[21] Michael Meyer described Keyes' attachment to his grandfather in a memoir published in *Windmill* in 1944: 'The memory of his grandfather – a tempestuous old man – was to dominate his life. Other heroes displaced his grandfather – but he was the prototype'. The metaphysical sensitivity to death, the necessity of fighting Time, the need to connect with the past and with great men – these themes all make their first appearance in 'Elegy':

> April, again, and it is a year again
> Since you walked out and slammed the door
> Leaving us tangled in your words. Your brain
> Lives in the bank-book, and your eyes look up
> Laughing from the carpet on the floor:
> And we still drink from your silver cup.
>
> It is a year again since they poured
> The dumb ground into your mouth:
> And yet we know, by some recurring word
> Or look caught unawares, that you still drive
> Our thoughts like the smart cobs of your youth –
> When you and the world were alive.
>
> A year again, and we have fallen on bad times
> Since they gave you to the worms.
> I am ashamed to take delight in these rhymes
> Without grief; but you need no tears.
> We shall never forget nor escape you, nor make terms
> With your enemies, the swift departing years.
>
> July 1938

Sidney Keyes' early contact with suffering set him apart from a society which, he felt, defied his understanding and resisted his influence. Unlike an Alun Lewis who could at least evoke the 'clearer' visions of his Welsh childhood and extend a known solidarity to his pictures of barracks life, Keyes translated his ruptured childhood and adolescence into the sharp internal divisions which all critics have noted as a hall-mark of his poetry. His teacher, Tom Stavely, himself a poet, described the early Keyes:

> The shaping of his genius is very hard to put briefly into words. From the first there seems to have been a happy, if uneasy marriage between the two halves of his decidedly split personality. The innermost stronghold of his spirit held the memories of primordial world.[22]

Michael Meyer also detected a split, but between an outwardly happy Keyes and an inwardly anxious one. 'Fear and guilt ruled him from the first. . . . He retained the distorting eye which transforms everything that excites it into something grotesque and macabre.'[23] This duality increased as he grew older and eventually found its fullest expression in his war poems.

'Childhood is not a period in time, it is a state of mind', wrote Sidney Keyes in the essay 'Mexico' (1942). 'It is beyond wisdom and thought. It lives in images; and I think if there is a god, he lives in the same way. Childhood lives in images, and my childhood was in three men playing pool and a cow's horned skull.'[24] To a degree, Keyes always remained an inhabitant of this first world, an imaginative realm associated with visions of fate and death.

His highly self-conscious essay, 'Mexico', is not wholly trustworthy, even as his notebook entries can mislead;[25] yet the importance of the horned skull is borne out by the intensity with which he treats this image and by its recurrence in his poetry. In this essay, Keyes described playing on a dry river bed near his house where he would chase and kill lizards. One day he came upon a horned skull in between boulders. 'I looked down into the crevice, hoping for lizards, and found that hard white face and great eyeholes staring back at me. . . . Like some kind of prehistoric totem then it seemed, uncouth and bestial with its wide eyeholes . . . I felt I ought to worship it; or at least propitiate it in some way.' First he threw rocks at it, and then dug a hole and buried it. Over the horns, which still stuck out, he built a small cairn of stones. 'When it was all buried and hidden, I was very sorry to leave it, because I felt something belonging to me was stifled in the sand.' Keyes' fascination with bones and 'dead things full of a rotten vitality undesirable yet undeniable' was never quite buried. His own bestiality, the darker self of his split personality, was the main source of his poetic images and power. That inner world, full of spiritual demons and primitive totems, remained the all-important one, while the structured family life in Kent which he never experienced became an outer world which he desired but could not rebuild in time of war.

In 1940, at the age of eighteen, Sidney Keyes entered Queen's College, Oxford, to read History. Like Lewis, he produced poems before he entered the army, and until he enlisted in April 1942 he was an active member of the Oxford literary scene. During this period of time, Keyes attempted to make connections with those around him – creating a circle of friends which included Michael Meyer, Drummond Allison, John Heath-Stubbs, Milein Cosmann and Renée-Jane Scott. His withdrawn childhood had increased a need for affection and society.

However, his interest in the past also compelled Keyes to communicate with the literary living and dead. His intelligence was stirred by Shakespeare, Rilke, Racine, Baudelaire, Schiller, Koestler, and the macabre of such prose writers as Faulkner and Kafka. Like Keats, possessed of a mind which invited and entertained the voices and feelings of those who had preceded him, Sidney Keyes was an avid absorber of other writers. To the aesthetic sense of a Pater, he yoked the imagination of a Donne. The combination produced a sensibility attuned to the beautiful and the horrific aspects of the living and the dead. He wrote tributes or 'poems of connection' to such figures as Yeats, Klee, Clare, Wordsworth, and Woolf. These poems, all evidence of his protean imagination, are addressed to certain aspects of himself. Indeed we can divide his interests into three general categories: the macabre, the visionary, and the pastoral. Nine weeks before he died, Keyes contended that he should have been born in the nineteenth century in Wiltshire or Oxfordshire instead of near London between two wars,

> because then I might have been a good pastoral poet, instead of an uncomfortable metaphysical without roots. The trouble is, that a thing of beauty isn't a joy for ever to me; nor am I content

to imagine beauty is truth etc. All I know is that everything in a vague sort of way means something else, and I want desperately to find out *what*.[26]

Keyes seems to have conversed with the absent and dead more frequently than with the living and present. Remembered as being shy, introspective and intellectual, polite but not at ease with people, he nonetheless formed some intense relationships at Oxford. It was there he came under the powerful influence of John Heath-Stubbs, who shared his own interest in myth and literature. As a friend of both, Michael Meyer helpfully accounts for their relationship: 'Heath-Stubbs was able to trace for him the origins of Romanticism in the primitive legends, and its subsequent development through the Medieval and, eventually, Augustan poets'. At the same time, he widened Keyes' knowledge of poetic technique, which was not yet adequate for his complex ideas.[27] While at Oxford, Keyes developed his visionary side, exploring more fully his interest in the occult and paranormal. Under the influence of Heath-Stubbs, new characters seemed to enter his work.[28] 'Troll Kings', 'Glaucus', and 'Little Drawda' concern the waking of dead ghosts. Phantoms of Arthur, Guenever (*sic*), Lancelot, Alexander, Ragnar, Barbarossa, Attila and others helped Keyes to move into yet another realm of the immortal dead. Here he found membership in a stable group.

But the dead were not enough for Sidney Keyes, for he desperately needed relationships with the living. 'Time Will Not Grant' expresses his fears about impermanence and separation from those he loved – some of the famous dead with whom he links himself seem able to accept time's curses, but he cannot.

Time will not grant the unlined page
Completion or the hand respite
The Magi stray, the heavens rage,
The careful pilgrim stumbles in the night.

Take pen, take eye and etch
Your vision on this unpropitious time;
Faces are fluid, actions never reach
Perfection but in reflex or in rhyme.

Take now, now soon; your lost
Minutes roost home like curses.
Nicolo, Martin, every unhoused ghost
Proclaims time's strange reverses.

Fear was Donne's peace; to him
Charted between the minstrel cherubim,
Terror was decent. Rilke tenderly

Accepted autumn like a rooted tree.
But I am frightened after every good day
That all my life must change and fall away.

The yielding acceptance that Rilke practised was an ideal for
Keyes because it implied a humbling of the spirit which he was
often incapable of making. He could be as proud with those
around him as with Time. And while his hunger for love was
great, it often manifested itself in a possessive urge, rather than in
an easy acceptance of what another might share with him. Just as
he yearned for literary mothers and fathers to replace absent
parents, and needed the structure of a tradition, so he demanded
controlling authority in personal relationships. Forced into a war
where he was no more than victim or pawn, Keyes often dwelled
on another sort of battle where he had more control: love. 'Not
Chosen', for instance, commemorates the end of a love affair with
Milein Cosmann, but Keyes does not really accept a closing. 'O
take me back, but as you take remember / My love will bring
nothing but trouble, my dear.' 'Song: the Heart's Assurance',
another poem about Milein, depicts the self-distrust and cynicism
that grew from his innocent yet demanding love for her.

O never trust the heart's assurance –
Trust only the heart's fear;
. . .
For the careless heart is bound with chains
And terribly cast down:
The beast of pride is hunted out
And baited through the town.

Keyes' poems of love are poems of conflict, part of a war that runs
through all of his poetry. 'Love is to me, like everything else', he

confessed to Renée-Jane Scott in October 1942, 'a sort of battle, and one that never brings any victory, but only unrest and passion.'

Just before leaving Oxford, Keyes wrote a poem called 'The Foreign Gate' which unites the themes of love, war, and death in a new way. Here, death is not a ghost but an active Being who strips both lover and soldier. The death of the soldier is as difficult as the death of the lover, but because of the warrior's sacrifice to a greater cause, he can gain a certain nobility.

> There's no prescribed or easy word
> For dissolution in the Army books.
> The uniform of pain with pain put on is straiter
> Than any lover's garment; yet the death
> Of these is different, and their glory greater.
>   . . .
> Whatever gift, it is the giving
> Remains significant: whatever death
> It is the dying matters.
>   Emblematic
> Bronze eagle or bright banner or carved name
> Of fighting ancestor; these never pardon
> The pain and sorrow. It is the dying pardons
> For something different from man or emblem.
> Then drape the soldier's drum
> And carry him down
> Beyond the moon's inspection, and the noise
> Of bands and banners and the striking sun.
>
> Scatter the soldier's emblems and his fame:
> Shroud up the shattered face, the empty name;
> Speak out the word and drape the drum and spare
> The captive brain, the feet that walk to war
> The ironbound brain, the hand unskilled in war
> The shrinking brain, sick of an inner war.

Keyes held up publication of his first volume, *The Iron Laurel* (1942), in order to include 'The Foreign Gate'. It appears that he wished to sum up the 'ghostly battles' in which he had been a warrior/lover as he stepped closer to the real battlefield. Now his inner war would find its mirror image in real life.

In the army, Keyes' feelings of being surrounded by enemies intensified. 'At this moment', he confided to Milein Cosmann with whom he did not stop corresponding, 'I would like to reject the whole outer world, even to destroy it; another time I feel something resembling physical desire for it. The right way lies between these two: until I find it, this acute unrest will continue.'[29] The poem 'Anarchy' expresses most clearly the division of spirit which haunted Keyes:

> Rising the light ran round inside his eyes.
> Then at a later hour, without surprise
> He noted singing birds that raked the sky
> With pointed rods of sound like surgeon's knives.
>
> The walls were scrawled with moss. The trees
> Grabbed at the sun like grey anemones.
> At noon he met a girl whose body sang
> Thin as a cricket till his eardrums rang.
>
> Black dancers crossed his brain. The bearded sun
> Whirled past him, locked with prancing Capricorn.
> A dog began to howl, until he cried
> It was too much. And then his wonder died.
>
> Evening found him lost but unafraid
> Surveying the wry landscape in his head.
> Night ravished him, and so was brought to birth
> A great cold passion to destroy the earth.
>
> > March 1942

'Anarchy' records the birth of an inner violence aimed at destruction. At first this urge is expressed by a perverted natural world. Singing birds become rakers of the sky. Their pointed rods of sound scrape like cutting knives of surgeons. Like flowers, trees reach and grab for the sun, but as though they would blot out the light. The girl of line 7 and the black dancers of line 9 allude to a love affair with Milein and the sexual love and passion that sent Keyes nearly mad with frustration. Love unreturned seemed to end in a death of beauty for him. Song has been distorted into harsh and then ringing sounds, finally to end in a bestial howl.

When he verbalizes his pain in line 12 'it was too much' he is in fact already abandoned and lost. Raped by night and inner darkness, his passion turns from love to a possessive urge for destruction.

In the Army, Keyes could experience these feelings differently, for his hatred of the Army and the fact of war itself set in relief the inner divisions he had experienced throughout life. In a letter to Milein of June 1942, he was particularly direct:

> I was never bored until I joined the Army; now I am crazy with the utter futility, destructiveness and emptiness of my life, to which I see no end . . . As you see I'm not at all unhappy, but terribly disturbed. But I don't think you will see any change in me; the only difference is that now I am haunted by the chaos of the outer world, more than by my own personal world.

The poems published posthumously in *The Cruel Solstice* (1944) are requiems for peaceful England, laments for broken relationships, and attempts at confronting despair. In April 1943 in North Africa near Sidi Abdulla, Sidney Keyes failed to return from patrol. He was back from the Front on a demolitions course and was reported missing in action. It was not established whether he was shot immediately, or taken prisoner and executed. His grave was reported found at Massicault. Keyes had entered war as a man looking 'for peace' who found 'his own eyes barbed' ('War Poet'). He left it having faced his own destructiveness and pride as projected onto the fields of history. In letters and in poems, he wrote of the necessity of every soldier to face death directly and accept it. On the battlefield he, like Orestes in his 'Orestes and the Furies', met and faced his private and public destinies.

In January 1939 Keyes had written a dream poem which helps illuminate his very last production: 'The Wilderness'. 'Meditation of Phlebas the Phoenician', he wrote, 'has no meaning'; yet its narrator is a corpse who wishes to remain drowned. 'Why must I go? I am a corpse long-drowned.' Keyes did not really want to be a warrior; yet by going to war and facing death, his own inner turmoil became more real. As Meyer wrote, imagination and reality became one. He did not remain in the world of the imagination, writing elegies in the autumn landscapes of Kent or Oxfordshire. Rather he faced the present though he continued to see it in wholly personal terms. 'The Wilderness' marks a climax in Keyes' development. In this extract he says farewell to both childhood and the pride he felt he had manifested in love relationships:

The Wilderness

Here where the horned skulls mark the limit
Of instinct and intransigent desire
I beat against the rough-tongued wind
Toward the heart of fire.

So knowing my youth which was yesterday,
And my pride which shall be gone tomorrow,
I turn my face to the sun, remembering gardens
Planted by others – Longinus, Guillaume de Lorris
And all love's gardeners, in an early May.

O sing, small ancient bird, for I am going
Into the sun's garden, the red rock desert
I have dreamt of and desired more than the lilac's promise.
The flowers of the rock shall never fall.

O speak no more of love and death
And speak no word of sorrow:
My anger's eaten up my pride
And both shall die tomorrow.

Knowing I am no lover, but destroyer,
I am content to face the destroying sun.

In 'The Wilderness' and the poem preceding it, 'The Grail', Keyes was moving towards a more religious and universal stance with an emphasis on sacrifice which he had only started to define in earlier poems. But sacrifice was not for Keyes what it was for Lewis. It was not a death wish, a slip into the embrace of nothingness. Rather, it was linked with an active spiritual principle practised in life by other visionaries. It had nothing to do with possession of the world. As Keyes said: 'Wordsworth and Rilke were not troubled by this violent need for possession'[30] but rather acceptance of one's failings and of the challenges sent by God. Keyes sees death as he saw life, as a battle. Echoes of T. S. Eliot's *The Waste Land* and *Little Gidding* permeate 'The Wilderness'. However, the poem acts as more than a compendium of other works which house a religious spirit and as more than the climax of Keyes' spiritual biography. It also calls to his fellow men, and transcends the personal.

In an essay 'The Artist in Society' (1942) Keyes expressed his belief that the artist has a special purpose in society. He alone can revitalize the relationship between temporal and eternal. The work of the best artist will, he wrote:

> bear only the same relation to his vision as shorthand does to speech; but he will have succeeded, as far as possible, if he can give to his audience some inkling of the continual fusion of finite and infinite, spiritual and physical, which is our world; if he can to some extent express the eternal meaning which resides in the physical world, and can show the relationship between the eternal and its physical counterpart. He will see not only 'eternity in a grain of sand' but the grain of sand as an eternal part of eternity.

It is impossible to predict whether or not Keyes would have developed poetically after the war, or in what direction. What remains, two volumes of verse produced in six years, is a remarkable poetic achievement for a man of only twenty-one.

Ronald Blythe named Keyes as 'the most important and prolific of the Second World War poets in his anthology *Components of the Scene*.[31] Reviews of Keyes' work at the time were highly favourable and he was awarded the Hawthornden Prize posthumously in 1944. Keyes' prodigious talent is not unique among young poets; yet added to his achievement is the fact that he perfectly reflected the deep tensions and anxieties of his time. He turned inward like so many other writers and confronted the demons of the private self. Yet he won public fame soon and was enshrined as a sacrificial victim, like the golden-haired Rupert Brooke of the First World War. That such a private and literary voice was accorded rich public honour attests to his special representativeness for the intellectuals of the Second World War. A poet of death and battle from the very beginning, Keyes did not have to wait long for the world to provide the exact arena for his talent. Keyes survived in poetry when others failed or were deterred because he was able to wed his imaginative world to the circumstances around him.

Both Lewis and Keyes were pacifists by nature, but while Lewis remained indecisive about his role in war, Keyes felt forced into activism by historical necessity. Viewing war as an interruption to his home life and career, Lewis avoided taking sides. Yet, recalling his homeland, he projected the injustices done to his family as a class in Wales onto class divisions in the army and onto the peasants of India. In so doing, he achieved fine realistic portraits in prose and poetry. Lonely, bored and displaced, Lewis yearned to return to a former time and landscape. More and more alienated from life itself, and of too practical a nature to yield completely to the spiritual, he died seeking to make the world more 'loving'. Paradoxically, Lewis yielded to a Lamia-like embrace of death, divesting himself of the social responsibilities he had flirted with, while the private visionary Keyes became a social martyr.

Where Lewis saw battle as an undesirable necessity, Keyes gripped that necessity as a test of personal courage. He imaginatively wrote of his own personal devils – pride and destructiveness – set in relief by war, with an authority gained from literary fathers. Where Lewis achieved a poetry of refusal, Keyes wrote a poetry of connection, connection of himself to others and of the physical to the spiritual. Though often distanced from real battles by myth or literary overlay, his poems strongly lament the current stage in the history of man. They are epitaphs 'for (those of) us who must be anarchists because the age is against us'.[32] The age was against Keyes and he would make no terms in battle with it. His desire to understand the spiritual structure behind the world compelled Keyes to view self-sacrifice and acceptance as the highest forms of love and honour.

NOTES

1. See the following contemporary evaluations: Robert Graves, 'War Poetry', *The Listener*, 21 October 1941, p. 567; Michael Meyer, 'Sidney Keyes: A Memoir', *The Windmill*, I, 1944, p. 58; Henry Reed, 'Poetry in War Time: The Younger Poets', *The Listener*, 25 January 1945, pp. 100–1; Michael Meyer, Introduction to *The Collected Poems of Sidney Keyes* (London: Routledge, 1945); J. Maclaren-Ross, 'Second Lieutenant Alun Lewis', *Penguin New Writing*, 27 (April 1946) pp. 78–80. A. L. Rowse, introduction to Lewis' *Letters from India* (Cardiff: Penmark Press, 1946); Tom Stavely, 'The Boyhood of a Poet', *The Listener*, 23 January 1947, pp. 162–3. Also see the

helpful summary of major reviews on the posthumous work of Keyes in John
Guenther, *Sidney Keyes* (London: Editions Poetry London, 1967) pp. 208–11.
He quotes reviews by Vita Sackville-West, Harold Nicolson, Richard
Church and A. L. Rowse. References to Keyes, Lewis (and Douglas) as the
important war poets are scattered through pamphlets exchanged in the
armed services such as *Khaki and Blue* (see Chapter 3, note 40).

2. Alun Lewis, Letter 30, to his parents, *Letters from India*, p. 73.
3. Alun Lewis, quoted by Ian Hamilton, Introduction to *Alun Lewis, Selected
Poetry and Prose* (London: George Allen and Unwin, 1966) p. 44.
4. Lewis, Letter 11, *Letters from India*, p. 49.
5. Hamilton, Introduction to *Alun Lewis, Selected Poetry and Prose*, p. 11.
6. Ibid., p. 19.
7. Published in *Selected Poetry and Prose*, pp. 185–201.
8. Hamilton, Introduction, p. 13.
9. Quoted by Hamilton who had access to letters and the unpublished journal,
p. 19.
10. Samuel Hynes, *The Auden Generation* (London: Bodley Head, 1976) p. 191.
11. Alun John, *Alun Lewis* (Cardiff: University of Wales Press, 1970) p. 84.
12. John Stuart Williams, 'The Poetry of Alun Lewis', *Anglo-Welsh Review*, XIV,
33 (1964–5) p. 60.
13. Williams, in 'The Poetry of Alun Lewis', asserts that the lyric and short story
are more alike than they really are, p. 59.
14. Hamilton, letter to Richard Mills, November 1941, p. 35.
15. Ibid., p. 32.
16. Quoted in Stefan Schimanski and Henry Treece (eds), *Leaves in the Storm*
(London: Lindsay Drummond, 1947) p. 72.
17. Hamilton, from the unpublished journals, p. 40.
18. Ibid., p. 41.
19. John Lehmann, 'A Human Standpoint', in *The Open Night* (New York:
Harcourt Brace, 1952) p. 111.
20. Robert Hewison, *Under Siege* (London: Weidenfeld & Nicolson, 1977) p. 123.
21. Sidney Keyes, in the Introduction to *Eight Oxford Poets*, p. viii.
22. Stavely, 'The Boyhood of a Poet', p. 162.
23. Meyer, 'Sidney Keyes: A Memoir', p. 58.
24. 'Mexico' is to be found in Michael Meyer (ed.), *Minos of Crete:* plays and
stories by Sidney Keyes with selections from his notebook and letters; and
some early unpublished poems (London: Routledge, 1945) pp. 134–5.
25. *Minos of Crete*, in section 'Notebook 1942–3', p. 153. 'This is not written for
posterity', Keyes writes, 'but for my own interest. But as I am a poet, I am
not honest in writing, and must be supposed to have an eye (even a
subconscious one) on the printed page.'
26. Quoted by Meyer, Introduction to *The Collected Poems of Sidney Keyes*, p. xiii in
the un-numbered footnote.
27. Ibid.
28. Guenther, *Sidney Keyes*, p. 60.
29. Quoted by Guenther.
30. *Minos of Crete*, in section 'Selections from Letters', p. 177.
31. Ronald Blythe, *Components of the Scene* (Harmondsworth: Penguin, 1966) p.
15.

32. Sidney Keyes, letter to Renée-Jane Scott, 26 July 1942, quoted in Guenther, *Sidney Keyes*, p. 123. Also see his letter to Milein Cosmann of 21 June 1942: 'If my values – or ours – conflict with those of the age, we must never doubt that the age is mistaken, not ourselves', quoted by Michael Meyer in *Minos of Crete*, p. 177.

5 No Enemy But Death: The Poetry of Keith Douglas

And death who had the soldier singled
has done the lover mortal hurt.   ('Vergissmeinnicht')

I

'Dear Grandpapa', wrote Keith Douglas at the age of six, 'I went
to a Fate yesterday and a consert too. I bought a gun for 4^d which
was marked 6^d at the toy shop there.'[1] In this fragment from a
letter of childhood, Keith Douglas naively reveals what would
become the most significant difference between himself and the
other major poets of the Second World War. For, attracted to the
military from his youth and schooled in its ways, Keith Douglas
gave himself gladly to the excitements and dangers of war. In a
schoolboy's analysis (possibly from 1932) he defined himself as a
'militarist' who 'like many of his warlike elders, built up heroic
opinions upon little information'.[2] While lamenting the brutality
of war, he still remained devoted to the Officers' Training Corps
and joined its Mounted Section for the free riding when he went
up to Oxford in the autumn term of 1938. An aristocratic
horseman and a courageous soldier by nature, Douglas also
possessed the finely complex sensibility of the artist. Already a
promising painter, he set out at fourteen to master the art of
poetry. The war of 1939–45 proved his fittest subject, and he was
its best poet.

More than Lewis or Keyes, Douglas was conscious of the given
attitudes towards war and military life. Brought up on stories of
combat, Douglas was known from his cadet days for his obsessive
attention to cleaning and polishing the accoutrements of his trade –

113

Keith Douglas as a cadet, 1940, with his own embellishments.

his uniform, saddle, bridle, boots, and so on. In a 1940 picture (see page 114) which shows him at ease in uniform, he stands tall with buttons and boots shining. Significantly enough, Douglas added an embellished decorative border to the picture with the caption: 'Dulce et decorum est pro patria mori'. The romantic hearts and flowers in the border suggest a certain sentimentality about the classically heroic line. Yet it can also be no accident that in his chosen caption Douglas should echo Wilfred Owen's sardonic use of Horace in his First World War poem, 'Dulce Et Decorum Est'. Even though he had not yet gone to battle, Douglas saw himself not only in the romantic tradition of great warriors, but also in the great chain of realistic modern war poets.

Like the poets of the First World War, Douglas ironically details the horror of the battlefield in his best and most famous poems, those written during and after his combat duty in the Middle East (autumn 1941–autumn 1943: Middle East; autumn 1943–April 1944: England and the Normandy Landings). His cynicism, as reflected in the following verses of 'Gallantry', brings to mind Sassoon's outraged tone:

> The Colonel in a casual voice
> spoke through the microphone a joke
> which through a hundred earphones broke
> into the ears of a doomed race.
>
> Conrad luckily survived the winter:
> he wrote a letter to welcome
> the auspicious spring: only his silken
> intentions severed with a single splinter.
>
> It was a brave thing the Colonel said,
> but the whole sky turned too hot
> and the three heroes never heard what
> it was, gone deaf with steel and lead.

The shattered beliefs of Sassoon and Owen are also recalled in poems which, like 'The Trumpet', express Douglas' near-despair over the brutality of war and the waning of aristocratic honour. The poem ends:

                                  We must be up early

tomorrow, to forget the cry and the crier
as we forgot the conversation
of our friends killed last month, last week
and hear, crouching, the air shriek
the crescendo, expectancy to elation
violently arriving. The trumpet is a liar.

Though he appears to act as a public spokesman, Douglas can
share neither the compassionate detachment of Owen nor the
need to penetrate civilian complacency, which is the hallmark of
Sassoon's poetry. He is closer to Isaac Rosenberg, who depicted
the victims of the battlefield as particularized instances of war's
outrage with a mixed response of anger and compassion.[3]

Douglas, too, writes a poetry of suffering, but strives for the
simultaneous expression of responses which go beyond mere pity.
He compels readers to look honestly at death, the corruption of
the Middle East, the barren desert. In 'Dead Men', written after
his participation in the battle of El Alamein, an eastern romanticism, associated with the unreliable yearnings of the heart,
becomes harshly displaced by a western reality. He has come to
identify this reality with the cruelties of war and with the old
tormentings of a private demon or 'beast' that haunts his poetry
from the very beginning:

Tonight the moon inveigles them
to love: they infer from her gaze
her tacit encouragement.
Tonight the white dresses and the jasmin scent
in the streets. I in another place
see the white dresses glimmer like moths. Come
to the west, out of that trance, my heart –
here the same hours have illumined
sleepers who are condemned or reprieved
and those whom their ambitions have deceived;
the dead men, whom the wind
powders till they are like dolls. . . .

In 'Cairo Jag', the 'jasmin scent' of 'Dead Men' has degenerated
into 'a stink of jasmin'. Still in

   streets dedicated to sleep
 stenches and the sour smells, the sour cries
 do not disturb their application to slumber
 all day. . . .

The speaker considers yielding to the sham realities of 'this
stained white town'. Feelings of lassitude, curiosity, revulsion,
and 'fatalism' become intermixed. What wins out in the end,
however, is Douglas' awareness of a locality, which, though cruel
and devoid of Cairo's mock-allurements, fascinates, as in 'Dead
Men', by the sheer force of its harsher honesty:

   But by a day's travelling you reach a new world
   the vegetation is of iron
   dead tanks, gun barrels split like celery
   the metal brambles have no flowers or berries
   and there are all sorts of manure, you can imagine
   the dead themselves, their boots, clothes and possessions
   clinging to the ground, a man with no head
   has a packet of chocolate and a souvenir of Tripoli.

By the sparse painting of the landscape and the dead, Douglas
actually tells us much, for he urges the reader to provide the full
significance of the details he offers – the sharpness of the metal, the
stench of the bodies, the whys of the chocolate and souvenir.
Unlike the poets of the First World War, Douglas refuses to shape
our responses. And unlike Lewis, who denies commitment and
intimacy, or Keyes, who engages in a colloquy with himself
though seeming to engage others, Douglas forces us to feel a range
of emotions as wide and deep as his own by the sheer accretion of
conflicting responses.

II

Keith Castellain Douglas was born in Tunbridge Wells, Kent, on
24 June 1920. From his youth he loved shapes and colours, then
words and images. An only child and independent, he actively
seized upon creative self-amusements. Placed in a boarding
school at the age of six because of family problems, Douglas
flourished in reading and writing early. When he was eight his

father, a career soldier, left the family to live with another woman, and Keith Douglas never saw him again. Like Sidney Keyes, Douglas was deeply affected by the broken relationships of his childhood, and they made their way directly into his war poetry. Similarly, Douglas was able to understand and grasp the complexities of war better for having been exposed early to suffering and disjunction.

Two images, expressed in various forms, weave in and out of Douglas' poems. The first is that of an uncaring father, a distanced God who governs men's lives and reduces them to puppets on the stage of life. The other major image is that of a beast 'so amorphous and powerful that he could be a deity'.[4] It seems clear that the two images of uncaring father and beast are related, outer and inner forms of the same ruling deity. Variously named as Devouring Time, Death, the beast, God, the power he describes is 'inefficient' or cruel. Implacably, this devilish manipulator breaks and severs the relationships that Douglas seeks. His strong response to its domination was exacerbated by his need for order, his attraction to justice, and the real absence of his father.

Douglas responded fully to the Second World War for complicated reasons. He loved the military order; he took pride in being a member of a group. But essentially he responded to the breakdown of structures and was drawn to the nobility inherent in the role of warrior. The reality of his youth and manhood was dominated by family severance and catastrophic national events. Even his poetic creed, found in an essay 'On the Nature of Poetry', which was printed in *Augury*[5] (the Oxford anthology of 1940 that he edited with Alec Hardie), stresses the ideals of honour and order:

> In its nature poetry is sincere and simple. Writing which is poetry must say what a writer has himself to say, not what he has observed others to say with effect, nor what he thinks will impress his hearers because it impressed him hearing it. Nor must he waste any more words over it than a mathematician: every word must work for its keep in prose, blank verse, or rhyme.

The passage reflects Douglas' independent spirit and his desire for sincerity, but above all it records his interest in structure. The parts of a poem, each single element, must join to the larger whole and work significantly for it. In an earlier age, Douglas might well have been a Rupert Brooke patriot; however, the hierarchical empire was dissolving and a lonely waste land was replacing it. It is probably no accident that Douglas' work appealed to T. S. Eliot,[6] for both men were interested in tradition, fusion, and structure. Both were also seekers for belief in an age providing none.

Douglas did not move, like Eliot, towards faith – perhaps because his experience of the 'boredom, the horror and the glory' of battle outstripped any of Eliot's mental demons, more likely because scepticism and doubt dominated any leanings towards faith. A devil constantly rides on Douglas' back. In a drawing he made in 1944 for the cover of a book he planned to call *Bête Noire*, a black devil clings to Douglas as he rides his horse. In other sketches, the 'monster' grips, claws and fells him. Douglas' battles are not only with outer forces but with inner ones, for he feels cut off from half of himself. The war did not cause his self-division, but it provided him with the opportunity to face the bestial landscapes of war in the Middle East and Europe and the monster within his aristocratic self. Like Keyes, he used war to explore the darker side of himself in personal terms, yet unlike Keyes he did not put faith in sacrifice. He responded fully to each experience, including death, and while moral, was not a moralizer.

Douglas' poetic development shows an increased understanding of these private struggles and a need to weld them to external events. The dualities noticed in 'Dead Men' and 'Cairo Jag' – dualities of landscape, and attitudes – were adumbrated in his earlier poems. From his Oxford days, in a poem such as 'Invaders', one detects a split in his psyche. There the duality is one of head and heart. 'Intelligences like black birds / come on their dire wings from Europe', threatening ominously to 'harden' sensitive hearts. Douglas warns an unidentified *you* who is himself as much as any reader: 'You will find, after a few tomorrows / like this, nothing will matter but the black birds.' Douglas comes out on the side of the heart, defending it against its struggle with trespassers who would rob it of the pleasures in beauty and order. The political allegory of this poem written in the eventful year of 1939 is overt; what is equally significant is the equation of foreign invaders with the mind's own scourging black birds. The birds are clearly forerunners of the black beast whom Douglas will describe as residing 'inside my mind'.[7] His only defence against the invaders, however, is to incorporate their perpetrations, to become as 'intelligent' as they are and fight them on their own terms. Douglas exhorts, 'To keep the heart still sensitive as air will be our part, always to think'. Though written at Oxford, 'Invaders' is a military poem. The black aggressors whom Douglas wants to repulse are, like the late enemy armies, already dimly perceived as integral elements of his own divided psyche.

In another early poem, 'Sanctuary' (1940), Douglas is more personal but again writes of invasion and the breakdown of the heart.

> Once my mother was a wall;
> behind my rampart and my keep
> in a safe and hungry house
> I lay as snug as winter mouse:
> till the walls break and I weep
> for simple reasons first of all.
>
> All the barriers give in,
> the world will lance at every point
> my unsteady heart, still and still
> to subjugate my tired will.
> When it's done they will anoint me,
> being kinder if they win.
>
> So beyond a desperate fence
> I'll cross where I shall not return,
> the line between indifference
> and my vulnerable mind:
> no more then kind or unkind
> touch me, no love nor hate burn.

The split between head and heart now is cast through the opposition of youth and age. One side of the speaker is the mother's child, the small and snug and loved 'mouse' who felt at one with his environment. But the child's safe world is destroyed. The child feels subjugated and as an adult grows more indifferent and unwilling to be as vulnerable as he once was. Yet though he crosses the fence and leaves the sanctuary behind, he does so reluctantly. For he still clings to the barriers which have fallen.

Two versions of the same poem, 'Soissons' and 'Soissons 1940', illustrate the duality in Douglas even more strongly. In the first version Douglas is as ironic and intellectual a speaker as the adult of 'Sanctuary' or the victim of 'Invaders'. He describes the religious sanctuary of Soissons as permeated by devils. The craftsman who would have made angels in 'the religious century' makes 'devils from the selfsame stone'. The poem is shot through with dark and sinister suggestions which go unexplained: 'Down the long hill snakes / the hard hot road into the town's heart' and 'How dark / seems the whole country we enter.' In this first version of 'Soissons' Douglas gives us a single tone and reality; yet his second version testifies to his realization that a single point of view is incorrect. He attempts to set right the first version: 'a simplified medieval view / taken from a Book of Hours'.

Douglas writes the second poem from a much more complex vantage point. By incorporating two points of view, he introduces what will become a hallmark of his war poetry. First he describes a real edifice:

> This town is no tower of the mind
> and the cathedral, not an edifice of air, stands
> dignified and sleepy with serenity –
> so I would have said, and that this solid city
> was built here close under the angels' hands,
> something we had no longer reckoned to find.

The cathedral is not airy but solid. Yet in stanza two, he admits that once it was insubstantial:

> Yet here something of the mind lived and died,
> a mental tower restored only to fall
> and we in England heard it come down
> as though of all, this was the most ominous sound.
> The devils pilloried in that holy wall
> must smile to see our faith broke to the wide.

By the second stanza the main theme of the poem, the crisis of belief, comes into focus. The solid structure is just a hollow shell of former faith. Douglas feels the need for that solid structure informed by belief, but he is forced to document its destruction. Where earlier he was content to give a simple view, here he dwells

on paradox and ambivalence. The last stanza leaves us unde-
cided, as is the author, about the relationship among God,
history, and believers:

> You who believe you have a kind creator
> are with your sire crowding into twilight,
> as using excellent smooth instruments,
> material man makes himself immense.
> Oh you may try, but can't deny he's right
> and what he does and destroys makes him greater.

No longer settling for one side, the poet accepts ambivalence and
incomplete understanding.

In these early poems, Douglas records his self-divisions which
took various forms: two aspects of the self in conflict, two realms
such as heart and intelligence, two systems such as Catholic
France and Protestant England. Not able to fuse the discordant
opposites, Douglas nonetheless persists in his need for some kind
of order. It is significant that many of his poems concern buildings
or walls. Just as on the border of the 1940 picture of himself in
uniform Douglas drew classical columns, so in these poems he
expresses the same desire for a structure of belief which will
survive. One of the key changes in 'Soissons 1940' from draft to
final version is the deletion of the word *survived* in line 8, 'a mental
tower restored only to fall' where it has been replaced by *restored*
(Add. MS. 53773). Even the structure itself is fragile and may be
rebuilt only to fall again.

III

War accentuated both the split that Douglas had come to feel and
his need to integrate the dualities of his psyche. But at first he was
sceptical about writing 'war poetry'. His gradual assumption of
the role of war poet becomes clearer when we look at an article he
wrote called 'Poets in this War', an important essay[8] that
develops an ideal also underlying his fine poem 'Desert Flowers'.
Like 'Cairo Jag', this essay was probably written in 1943, after
Douglas had experienced his first campaign of tank warfare. Here
Douglas recalls Brooke, Owen, Sassoon, Sorley and Rosenberg

and reminds us why they were able to capture in verse the unique nature of the First World War:

> Such was the jolt given to the whole conception men had had of the world and of war, and so clear was the nature of the cataclysm, that it was natural enough not only that poets should be stirred, but that they should know how to express themselves.

On surveying his own generation, however, Douglas finds no one to compare with the poets of that earlier cataclysmic war: 'I do not find even one who stands out as an individual'. Having dismissed various predecessors and contemporaries including recent colleagues who had 'sprung up among the horrors of wartime Oxford', Douglas tries to account for the dearth of poets writing about the war. The reasons he lists are psychological, military and strategic.

At the time Douglas wrote 'Poets in this War' he was experiencing some frustration in coming to terms with the war. For while he clearly felt a strong kinship with the First World War poets, he also recognized that all poets of the Second World War must inevitably be alienated from them. There *are* 'fighting' war poets among his contemporaries, he admits, but these 'do not write because there is nothing new, from a soldier's point of view about this war except its mobile character'. Given such a paucity of subject matter, it follows according to Douglas that 'almost all that a modern poet on active service is inspired to write would be tautological'.

Douglas' point of view was probably shared by other poets and helps to explain why some, like Keyes and Douglas himself, were driven to stress more personal issues. A despairing spirit, along with an awareness of the disjunction between poetry and politics, looms behind this essay. Such a separation may also explain the difficulties of a poet like Alun Lewis whose creative impulses were more social than personal. When Douglas closes his essay by referring to the poetry of this global war as 'civil and military', he refers to the bombing of Britain as well as to war abroad; yet he also calls attention to the key feature he shares with poets of the First World War, and also to a major difference. Like its predecessor, the Second World War involved a conflict between armed forces of hostile nations. Yet the average British soldier did not want to go to war; rather, like Alun Lewis, he felt torn by responsibility and desire. More than any previous war, the Second World War produced an internal 'civil' conflict, as the allied components within individual psyches often were drawn into friction and battles by a divided self. (In Douglas' case, self-division is apparent not only in the 1940 photograph and in poems discussed earlier, but also in drawings bordering on the schizophrenic.)

In setting down his generation's ideas about the relation between war and creativity and about the war poets who had preceded them, Douglas was not including himself among those who would shirk or postpone writing of the 1939–45 war. In fact, by his very authorship of the essay, he was dissociating himself from other poets. But by not publishing the essay he may possibly have indicated his doubt about its central point of view. *He* would write a poetry of war. While despairing of new themes, he was sharply aware of his own peculiar strengths – strengths that could and did allow him to write poetry capable of facing both the 'civil and military' conflicts without and within. In 'Desert Flowers', written like 'Poets in this War' in 1943, he maintains that he has something fresh and distinctive to say. Though the speaker at first purports only to duplicate what Rosenberg had already chronicled in poems of war, it soon becomes obvious that he also wants to remove himself from his predecessor. The dependent 'I' of the second line has become independent in lines 10, 13 and 15. This speaker clearly assesses himself as doing much more than corroborating an earlier vision:

> Living in a wide landscape are the flowers –
> Rosenberg I only repeat what you were saying –
> the shell and the hawk every hour
> are slaying man and jerboas, slaying
>
> the mind: but the body can fill
> the hungry flowers and the dogs who cry words
> at nights, the most hostile things of all.
> But that is not new. Each time the night discards
>
> draperies on the eyes and leaves the mind awake
> I look each side of the door of sleep
> for the little coin it will take
> to buy the secret I shall not keep.

I see men as trees suffering
or confound the detail and the horizon.
Lay the coin on my tongue and I will sing
of what the others never set eyes on.

As the logical outcome of Douglas' independence of his
predecessors and colleagues, 'Desert Flowers' executes the main
ideas of 'Poets in this War'. Death on the battlefield promises a
new vision for the poet whose eyes have been clouded. His new
theme will be an honest exploration of his own relationship to war,
battle and death.

Douglas was drawn magnetically to the stage of war 'where the
incredible things happen'. In his *Journal* (Add. MS. 53774) which
would become his prose account of war, *Alamein to Zem Zem*,
Douglas confided that: 'When I could order my thoughts and look
for more significant things than appearances, I still looked – I
cannot avoid it – for something decorative, poetic or dramatic'.[9]
He describes many sights of the battlefield in romantic terms:
'This scene with the silhouettes of men and turrets interrupted by
swirls of smoke and the sky lightening behind them, was to be
made familiar to me by many repetitions'.[10] Douglas gives an
account of one of these common scenes, a tank in flames,
mythologically: dark grey-blue smoke issues from the side of a
turret 'like the Goddess Sin springing from the left shoulder of
Satan'.[11] Bombs and a fighter plane are likened to raindrops and a
gliding bird: 'The silver body of the aeroplane was surrounded by
hundreds of little grey smudges, through which it sailed on
serenely. From it there fell away, slowly and gracefully, an
isolated shower of rain, a succession of glittering drops.'[12] In these
prose passages, Douglas attempts to tame the fury and terror of
war with similes involving comparisons to the familiar or beloved.

In his poetry of battle, however, he charts war's effect on
himself. It is there that he sees remorseless cruelty as a condition
not only of the physical landscape but also of man himself.
'Devils', written in 1942, most clearly shows Douglas' recognition
of a single evil, without and within. This discovery occurs in a vast
silence, a 'deceptive quiet' similar to that Douglas associated with
the desert, a torn yet honest landscape. It also recalls his *Journal*
description of tank warfare: 'The view from a moving tank is like
that in a camera obscura or silent film'.[13] The world seems silent

but is not; yet the world within (inside the tank or inside the mind)
is even noisier:

> Outside the usual crowd of devils
> are flying in the clouds, are running
> on the earth, imperceptibly spinning
> through the black air alive with evils
> and turning, diving in the wind's channels.
> Inside the unsubstantial wall
> these idiots of the mind can't hear
> the demons talking in the air
> who think my mind void. That's all;
> there'll be an alliance of devils if it fall.

Again Douglas struggles to keep apart two factions, but here
instead of imagining angels in combat with devils, he views his
mind as he had viewed his body: as a fortress infiltrated by devils.
Earlier divided, body and mind are now joined by the fact that
they are both attacked. Both are subjected to assaults by a group
of devils and angels. 'Devils' is a poem of confusion in which the
speaker is alone and unable to help himself against powerful
forces which now threaten to fell him for good.

In landscape poems '1', '2' and '3', Douglas attempts to define a
direct relationship to the figures of war, dead and alive. In
'Landscape with Figures 1' Douglas observes the battlefield from
the vantage point of an airplane and sees the same insect world
described by poets of the First World War. The plain is 'dotted':
'the sand vehicles / squashed dead or still entire, stunned / like
beetles: scattered wingcases and / legs, heads, show when the haze
settles'. Yet Douglas seems to reject as spurious any visions of
battle which are too romantic or distanced.

In 'Landscape with Figures 2' the spectator personally confronts dead bodies which 'wriggle' as mimes of life. They are
'stony actors' unable to conquer the reality of the play they
perform. Douglas records his own creative struggles with the
reality and unreality of war. He continues in 'Landscape with
Figures 3' to speak in theatrical terms but moves to centre stage
from his position of spectator in '1' and from a figure on 'the back
cloth' in '2':

I am the figure burning in hell
and the figure of the grave priest
observing everyone who passed
and that of the lover. I am all
the aimless pilgrims, the pedants and courtiers
more easily you believe me a pioneer
and a murdering villain without fear

                        . . .
I am all these and I am the craven
the remorseful the distressed
penitent: not passing from life to life
but all these angels and devils are driven
into my mind like beasts. I am possessed,
the house whose wall contains the dark strife
the arguments of hell with heaven.

                        ? April–September 1943

By splitting himself into actor and spectator in the drama, Douglas paradoxically is able to see himself in many more roles. He no longer pigeonholes himself or his poems into stereotyped combats of devils and angels, but forces a multiple point of view on himself, even as he had forced it on his reader in other poems. Now he is priest, penitent, killer, questor, victim; it bears noting that he will never again use *angel* in a poem.

Seeking to be more than an oracular poet – or one of the 'orators dropping down a curtain of rhetoric' ('The Offensive 2') – Douglas chooses to pull back the self-imposed draperies of man's eyes, to move from background to foreground, and openly confront his own complicated feelings toward destruction and self-destruction. War enabled Douglas to develop a new stage in his work. As he wrote to J. C. Hall in the summer of 1943, the lyricism of his early days was no longer viable after his active participation in battle.[14] While he was 'finished with one form of writing' and was 'progressing towards another', Douglas was grasping for a closer personal integration of conflicting internal impulses. He could no longer write in the lyrical 'old forms' Hall admired; he could write only 'true things'. Having faced war, he declared: 'Now I will write of it and perhaps one day cynic and lyric will meet and make me a balanced style'. Douglas could not succumb to a 'sentimental or emotional' reaction to war (though his very declaration proves how alluring lyricism was) but spoke

'Behind the Horseman Sits Black Care'; sketches by Keith Douglas for the cover of *Bête Noire*.

passionately for 'honesty' and some kind of belief even if that belief had to be tempered:

> To be sentimental or emotional now is dangerous to oneself and to others. To trust anyone or to admit any hope of a better world is criminally foolish, as foolish as it is to stop working for it. It sounds silly to say work without hope, but it can be done; it's only a form of insurance; it doesn't mean work hopelessly.

Like Lewis, Douglas was a realist, but like Keyes he was also a romantic who carried a beast within. In war, romantic and realist met. Douglas had realized that the new war poet could not be a patriotic national spokesman. Nor was there a need to teach the civilians about war or 'paint' specific war events. Rather, he understood that the Second World War poet carried his own demon into the realm of history and that his identity could be defined only by their interaction. Douglas looked upon war as a personal test and a battle with the devilish tormentor he called 'Bête Noire'.

Douglas dramatically documents the predominance of this beast in the drawings of February 1944 (see page 128) and in notes he made in connection with his volume of poetry called *Bête Noire*. In December of 1943, on leave to prepare for the invasion of Europe, Douglas had started work on a manuscript of his poems for Tambimuttu who had published some of them already in *Poetry (London)*. In February 1944 he received a contract with Editions Poetry London, and in March he had decided on the title. While rushing to select and order his poems, Douglas attempted versions of a new poem called by the same name as his volume. One draft names the beast 'my particular monster' and recognizes it as a permanent inhabitant for over ten years. Although Douglas fails to identify fully the nature of this beast, it seems to represent an asocial and destructive, or self-destructive, urge. In another version of this Ur-poem, Douglas feels the stifling power of the animal he cannot subdue or yield to:

> The beast is a jailer
> allows me out on patrol
> brings me back by telepathy
> is inside my mind
> breaks into my conversations with his own words

speaking out of my mouth
can overthrow me in a moment
writes what I write, or edits it (censors it)
takes a dislike to my friends and sets me against them
. . .
If this is a game, it's past half time and the beast is winning.

After five fragmentary attempts, *Bête Noire* proved to be intractable material. And yet, like the childhood images of Sidney Keyes, the black monster-devil of Douglas' mind had already had a positive influence. '*Bête Noire*', he wrote in a 'Note for the Jacket of *Bête Noire*', 'is the name of the poem I can't write: a protracted failure, which is also a protracted success I suppose. Because it is the poem I begin to write in a lot of other poems: this is what justifies my use of that title for the book.'[15] Douglas died on 9 June 1944 in Normandy. After a successful patrol to ascertain enemy strength in the village of St Pierre, near Bayeux, Douglas moved with his regiment in tanks to the village square. Running to make his report, Douglas was hit by an explosion of heavy mortar fire. A small shell fragment must have hit him, for although there was no mark on his body, he died instantly.[16] He never conquered the beast nor was he able to complete his book. But his personal struggle with this monster paralleled and influenced his search for an idiom of modern war poetry – one both free of lyrical romanticism and excessive detail and yet more personal than public.

IV

The climax of Douglas' movement towards welding two sides of himself and integrating his personal struggles with history, is reached in his most famous poem 'Vergissmeinnicht'. There he is able to project fully his own internal battles onto the outer landscape of death by identifying himself with the enemy. Written in Tunisia in 1943, when Douglas' regiment was resting, 'Vergissmeinnicht' gains from being a poem of rediscovery and remembrance, a poem which moves from the common scenes of war to the more particularized and intimate instance of *one* dead man. Douglas discovers the body of a soldier, the same fighter who, like a demon, had fired at his tank in the warfare three weeks before. What remains of him now are the picture of his girlfriend and his utilitarian weapons, emblems of Eros and Mars:

> Three weeks gone and the combatants gone
> returning over the nightmare ground
> we found the place again, and found
> the soldier sprawling in the sun.
>
> The frowning barrel of his gun
> overshadowing. As we came on
> that day, he hit my tank with one
> like the entry of a demon.
>
> Look. Here in the gunpit spoil
> the dishonoured picture of his girl
> who has put: *Steffi. Vergissmeinnicht.*
> In a copybook gothic script.
>
> We see him almost with content,
> abased, and seeming to have paid
> and mocked at by his own equipment
> that's hard and good when he's decayed.
>
> But she would weep to see today
> how on his skin the swart flies move;
> the dust upon the paper eye
> and the burst stomach like a cave.
>
> For here the lover and killer are mingled
> who had one body and one heart.
> And death who had the soldier singled
> has done the lover mortal hurt.
>
> > (Tunisia May/June 1943)

Like others of his complicated poems, 'Vergissmeinnicht' refuses to allow the reader one reaction. It is not simply a recognition scene, nor is it carrying the message of a conciliatory Whitman: 'For my enemy is dead, a man as divine as myself is dead'.[17] At first the speaker is glad to see the enemy abused by death, but this contentment is too easy. Gradually, tenderness develops in the poem with the introduction of the enemy's beloved who 'would weep' if she could see the broken body of her man. Yet dwelling only for a moment on the 'dishonoured' picture of the German girl, Douglas withholds expressions of direct compassion and uses sparingly any phrases or words which would elicit pity. 'She would weep' distances the speaker's and the reader's involvements by making the crying come from another person, and conditionally at that. The literary and half-romantic *swart* is a touch of beauty which saves stanza 5 from becoming totally disgusting. It is, nevertheless, reduced to objective realism by modifying *flies*. It is just such a cautious interweaving of romantic touches with realism that complicates our response. Like Douglas, we are deeply moved by the scene before us; yet we are not allowed any self-deceptions.

Douglas exercises strict control over the material and over our responses, from the first stanza to the final antithetical closing. At first we see the soldier with the sun falling on his body. Then in its decay, as we follow directions and 'look' closer, we confront a paper eye and a stomach burst open like a giant hole. Beside him lies the picture of his girl. Yet perhaps the most important point about 'Vergissmeinnicht' is that the man is not a stereotype, even though the opening stanza with its slow and repetitive movement conditions us for a stereotyped war scene – the tank rolls slowly over ground travelled before. 'Look', which means 'look closer', is the most important single word in the poem. This enemy soldier is not just a German; he is 'Steffi', a man who loved a girl and who died in battle with Douglas.

Douglas fictionalizes the scene by his choice of words and by the progression of his images; he invests personal life with care into a common war occurrence. The fact that he understates his feelings, that all is given with the minimum of active involvement, stresses the power of his and our identification. The soldier is presented as killer, then as lover, but the last stanza shows the vulnerability of both such roles before Death. Douglas joins the personal with history here by his own self-projection; for in the last stanza, even as he speaks of the German soldier, he speaks primarily of himself:

> For here the lover and killer are mingled
> who had one body and one heart.
> And death who had the soldier singled
> has done the lover mortal hurt.

The killer and lover are yet another antithetical pairing of Douglas' beast/devil and angel/romantic. By his understanding that they mingle inextricably, he acknowledges their relationship: by inflicting mortal hurt on another, one kills the essentially human part of oneself and becomes no better than the beast. The lover here represents all that is human, moral, and personal; the killer is the inhuman, immoral and impersonal. Yet they are one.

Douglas' earlier poem 'The Prisoner' provides a valuable contrast to 'Vergissmeinnicht'. Written in 1940 at Sandhurst, the poem is addressed to a woman Douglas loved at Oxford:

> Today, Cheng, I touched your face
> with two fingers, as a gesture of love
> for I can never prove enough
> by sight or sense your strange grace;
>
> but like moths my hands return
> to your skin, that's luminous
> like a lamp in a paper house,
> and touch, to teach love and learn.
>
> I think a thousand hours are gone
> that so, like gods, we'd occupy:
> but alas, Cheng, I cannot tell why,
> today I touched a mask stretched on the stone-
>
> hard face of death. There was the urge
> to escape the bright flesh and emerge
> of the ambitious cruel bone.

The poem illustrates rather startlingly the reverse of Douglas' superimposition of love on death, as in 'Vergissmeinnich'. Here he applies the face of death, a skull, to the face of a lovely living human. A sketch of a divided face, half-woman, half-skull and skeleton belongs with this poem (see page 134). But in 'Vergissmeinnicht' Douglas does not have to provide a mask of death, a corpse or skull. The battlefield provides the scene of death, and he is able to draw something vital from it – a poem of rediscovery (the body), discovery (the photograph), and remembrance. While the war scene is responsible for the reversal, Douglas' ability to divide himself into spectator and actor is

Keith Douglas' illustration for 'The Prisoner'.

equally important. He becomes that German, lying dead, in a far more personal way than he ever relates to Cheng. In the later poem, he realizes that he has killed a part of himself.

Douglas truly becomes, with 'Vergissmeinnicht', a poet for whom literary history and geo-political history match: stereotypical boundaries are broken down. In the poems of 1943 boundaries between himself and others are dissolved by his declaration of himself as outcast, killer, lover, victim, brother, Jew, German, corpse. 'Vergissmeinnicht' is the culmination of that development towards a greater humanity. His poetry is not just that of a broken landscape or an exiled destroyed heart, but that of a civil war in which he sees and plays both sides. While Lewis could not commit himself to another and Keyes did not extend his poems of connection to the battlefield, Douglas recognizes that there is no enemy named Germany; its name is Death.

In his poem 'How to Kill', one of the last poems written in the Middle East, Douglas spoke again, but in a very different tone of the self-destruction involved in killing. This time he depicts a dehumanized soldier who seems to have become a professional killer. In the first stanza, Douglas compares the soldier's bullet with the gravity of a child's ball. Killing seems to be child's play; yet as the killer aims he knows the full meaning of his skill. He shatters an object of love with hatred:

> Now in my dial of glass appears
> the soldier who is going to die.
> He smiles, and moves about in ways
> his mother knows, habits of his.
> The wires touch his face: I cry
> NOW. Death, like a familiar, hears
>
> and look, has made a man of dust
> of a man of flesh. This sorcery
> I do. Being damned, I am amused
> to see the centre of love diffused
> and the waves of love travel into vacancy.
> How easy it is to make a ghost.
>
> . . .

In draft form, 'How to Kill' included the theme of Douglas' own death. In the final version he assumes the role of killer – his only victimization is due to damnation by some power he cannot know or explain.

V

The beast of Douglas' personal life seems to have made possible the fusions he managed in the 1943 poems, for it embodied the same destructive force as war itself. The beast had occurred earlier in various forms. Gradually it emerged to drive away or tame his early romantic lyricism. Douglas grew in poetic power when he faced war directly, for there he saw vividly the face of the same beast whose proximity he had formerly only sensed.

Like Keyes, Douglas felt doomed to early death. While in England in early 1944, before his regiment left for the Normandy landings in April, Douglas gave away his watch, seemed to lose interest in soldiering, and told various people that he would not survive.[18] His last poem is amazing in its calm acceptance and foreknowledge, amazing but not unexpected. In draft form it explored several possibilities the future might hold: a woman's lips, islands, a land beyond mountains, death. These were objects of a quest and a new stage in his life. The completed poem, 'On a Return from Egypt', concerns the unknown future, but it does not entertain multiple possibilities for that future:

> To stand here in the wings of Europe
> disheartened, I have come away
> from the sick land where in the sun lay
> the gentle sloe-eyed murderers
> of themselves, exquisites under a curse;
> here to exercise my depleted fury.
>
> For the heart is a coal, growing colder
> when jewelled cerulean seas change
> into grey rocks, grey water-fringe,
> sea and sky altering like a cloth
> till colour and sheen are gone both:
> cold is an opiate of the soldier.
>
> And all my endeavours are unluckly explorers
> come back, abandoning the expedition;
> the specimens, the lilies of ambition
> still spring in their climate, still unpicked:
> but time, time is all I lacked
> to find them, as the great collectors before me.

> The next month, then, is a window
> and with a crash I'll split the glass.
> Behind it stands one I must kiss,
> person of love or death
> a person or a wraith,
> I fear what I shall find.
>
> (England March/April 1944)

In the final version Douglas has put aside speculations in favour of
readiness. The quest in the poem is over, a retrospective, and not
something being undertaken now. The courage of the last stanza,
predominating over any fear, recalls an earlier poem 'Aristocrats'.
Echoing Roncesvalles in its last line ('I think with their famous
unconcern. / It is not gunfire I hear, but a hunting horn.'),
'Aristocrats' stands in the corpus as the epitome of Douglas'
aristocratic morality. In that poem he celebrates the nobility of
warriors riding to destruction, whether on horses or in tanks. He is
one of them:

> How can I live among this gentle
> obsolescent breed of heroes, and not weep?
> Unicorns, almost,
> for they are fading into two legends
> in which their stupidity and chivalry
> are celebrated. Each, fool and hero, will be an immortal.

As he faced every battle and his personal demons with courage
and honesty, so he faces death in 'On a Return from Egypt'. Life
for Douglas meant embracing one's destiny with an unflinching
nobility of spirit. He approved of responsiveness but not of
sentimentality, so it seems right to close with another poem about
his own death which, though written much earlier in his swift
poetic career, as early as 1941, is totally free from any self-
aggrandizement. A rewriting of Rupert Brooke's romantic 1915
poem 'The Soldier', 'Simplify Me When I'm Dead' is the farewell
of a soldier-poet going off to global war, the experience of his
generation. 'Simplify' may seem an odd command from a poet
who deals with complex reactions, but it does not mean reduce the
quality of response. Douglas asks us to strip away pretensions,
stereotypes, and any ideal images we may harbour. By asking to
be simplified in death, he forces honesty on the living. He wishes

time to judge him fairly; he will not abide the considerations of momentary hates or loves. Recalling Shakespeare and Yeats, and the humanity of Lear, Douglas recognizes the sweet and pure aristocracy of nakedness. As the poem strips itself down, it ends as it began. In death, Douglas is part of the natural order, no more and no less:

> Remember me when I am dead
> and simplify me when I'm dead.
>
> As the processes of earth
> strip off the colour and the skin
> take the brown hair and blue eye
>
> and leave me simpler than at birth,
> when hairless I came howling in
> as the moon came in the cold sky.
>
> Of my skeleton perhaps
> so stripped, a learned man will say
> 'He was of such a type and intelligence,' no more.
>
> Thus when in a year collapse
> particular memories, you may
> deduce, from the long pain I bore
>
> the opinions I held, who was my foe
> and what I left, even my appearance
> but incidents will be no guide.
>
> Time's wrong-way telescope will show
> a minute man ten years hence
> and by distance simplified.
>
> Through that lens see if I seem
> substance or nothing: of the world
> deserving mention or charitable oblivion
>
> not by momentary spleen
> or love into decision hurled,
> leisurely arrive at an opinion.
>
> Remember me when I am dead
> and simplify me when I'm dead.

NOTES

All quotations from poems come from Desmond Graham (ed.), *The Complete Poems of Keith Douglas* (Oxford: Oxford University Press, 1979). Variants are listed on pp. 127–42.

1. Keith Douglas, letter to his grandfather, 1926, Add. MS 56355.
2. Keith Douglas, quoted in Desmond Graham, *Keith Douglas, 1920–44, A Biography* (Oxford: Oxford University Press, 1974) p. 1.
3. See Jon Silkin's introduction to his anthology *The Penguin Book of First World War Poetry* (Harmondsworth: Penguin Books, 1979) esp. pp. 29 and 30.
4. Keith Douglas, 'Note on Drawing for the Jacket of *Bête Noire*', in Graham (ed.), *The Complete Poems of Keith Douglas*, p. 120.
5. Keith Douglas, 'On the Nature of Poetry', *Augury: An Oxford Miscellany of Prose and Verse* (Oxford: Blackwell, 1940) p. 38. Reprinted in G. S. Fraser, John Waller and J. C. Hall (eds), *The Collected Poems* (London: Editions Poetry London, 1951) p. 138 and in Graham (ed.), *The Complete Poems of Keith Douglas*, p. 123.
6. The fullest account of the Douglas/Eliot correspondence of 1941 is to be found in 'T. S. Eliot and Keith Douglas', by Antony Coleman, *The TLS* (2 July 1970) p. 731. Poems bearing Eliot's comments are located in the British Library Manuscript Division (Add. MS 53773).
7. Keith Douglas, 'The *Bête Noire* Fragments – Fragment B', *The Complete Poems*, p. 118.
8. Keith Douglas, 'Poets in this War', Add. MS 53773. Reprinted in *TLS* (23 April 1971) p. 478.
9. Keith Douglas, *Journal*, Add. MS 53774, p. 1. The journal was printed as *Alamein to Zem Zem* (London: Editions Poetry London, 1946). Also Faber & Faber, 1966; also Oxford University Press, 1979.
10. Keith Douglas, *Journal*, p. 11.
11. Ibid., p. 103.
12. Ibid., p. 12.
13. Ibid.
14. Keith Douglas, letter to J. C. Hall, 10 August 1943, reprinted in Graham (ed.), *The Complete Poems of Keith Douglas*, p. 124.
15. Douglas, 'Note on Drawing for the Jacket of *Bête Noire*', p. 120.
16. Graham, *Keith Douglas*, p. 256.
17. Walt Whitman, 'Reconciliation', in F. DeWolfe Miller (ed.), *When Lilacs Last in the Door Yard Bloom'd: Sequel to Drum Taps (1865–6)*, a Facsimile Reproduction (Florida: Scholars Facsimiles and Reprints, 1959) p. 23.
18. Graham, *Keith Douglas*, p. 250.

Epilogue: The War's Legacy in Verse

It would be all too simple to make the 1940 encounter between Sidney Keyes and Philip Larkin in the Turl, Oxford, a symbolic confrontation between two antithetical types of poetry. Keyes, who would perish in North Africa in mysterious circumstances a mere three years later, slighted his Oxford contemporary when he launched *Eight Oxford Poets* (1941); Larkin, who remained in England for the duration of the war, would soon discard his Yeatsian trappings, renounce myth and dream, and move towards an anti-romantic platform of accurate statement. There in the snowy Oxford street stood the war's victim-to-be and the war's survivor-to-be, neo-romantic and anti-romantic, the poet of the 1940s and the poet of the 1950s. Were the two men even dimly aware of the symbolic opposition they were later made to enact? In 1964, looking back at their meeting in the Turl, Larkin, though remembering Keyes' huge Russian fur hat, recalled no dialogue of momentous proportions. In fact, he insisted that they had little, if anything, to say to each other.[1]

Larkin's reconstruction may well involve a pose of dismissiveness. Still, it helps underscore the fact that the differences between the poetry of the 1940s and that of the 1950s can be too easily exaggerated. As poems of Roy Fuller, G. S. Fraser, even Keyes himself amply prove, the 1940s were hardly engulfed in the unrestrained emotionalism that Larkin and his fellow Movement poets attributed to the decade. But in their prescriptions for the renewed health of English poetry, the writers of the Movement branded as 'romantic scribblers'[2] all the poets immediately before them. Blake Morrison, to be sure, declares that the Movement 'on the whole admired'[3] the work of Roy Fuller, Alun Lewis, Keith Douglas, and Henry Reed, writers whom they were capable of separating from the excoriated Dylan Thomas, David Gascoyne, Edith Sitwell and the poets (notably Henry Treece) who had been

140

included in the Apocalyptic anthology *The White Horseman* (1941).
Yet there seems little evidence for the 'admiration' Morrison
reports.

In fact, Philip Larkin, who emerged as the group's finest poet
and who continued to adhere to many of its original tenets,
condemned practically all of his twentieth-century forerunners.
Larkin's dicta about 'war poets' are especially noteworthy. In a
1963 review of Wilfred Owen's *Collected Poems*, edited by C. Day
Lewis, Larkin praised Owen as the only poet after Hardy who
could be read without a sense of bathos.[4] In his article, Larkin set
the stage for his praise of Owen by rejecting other war poets,
notably those who, like Keyes, Douglas, Lewis and Fuller, had
grappled personally with the realities of the Second World War:

> The first rank poet should ignore the squalid accidents of war:
> his vision should be powerful enough to disregard it. Admit-
> tedly war might come too close for this vision to be maintained.
> But it is still essentially irrelevant.

In his dismissal of war poetry, Larkin seems to be echoing
William Butler Yeats' 1936 indictment of the genre. Defending his
choices for *The Oxford Book of Modern Verse*, Yeats had declared,
'passive suffering is not a theme for poetry. . . . If war is necessary,
it is best to forget its suffering as we do the discomfort of fever.'[5]
Yet Larkin's rejection of war poetry was made on very different
grounds. Laying aside Yeats' remarks as 'fatuous', he stressed his
own attraction to the very suffering that a poet such as Owen had
universalized in his poetry. Owen wrote not about the historical
event of the First World War, said Larkin, but about 'all war', 'all
suffering', 'all waste'. After 1918 'these things continued and the
necessity for compassion with them'.[6]

Though drawn to the theme of suffering, Larkin nonetheless
persisted in ignoring the poets of the 1940s. In doing so, he
obliquely presented an apologia for his own creative avoidance of
the 'squalid accidents of war'. And he was certainly not alone in
his desire to repress the cataclysm. Yet his very attachment to
Owen and to the tradition of war poetry points to the continuing
influence of the 1940s in the literary climate of the 1950s. Larkin
professed to be especially moved by Owen's lines, 'there was a
quaking/of the aborted life within him leaping'. He thus singled
out the theme of 'undone years' – an obsession he shared with all

members of his war-haunted generation, including the Sidney Keyes he had met in the Turl.

I   1940 TO THE EARLY 1950s: PERSONAL ORIGINS OF THE MOVEMENT

Just as the early friendships of Keyes, Douglas, Allison, Meyer, and Heath-Stubbs influenced the values and aims of poets on the eve of war, so other concurrent friendships, originating in the same years, yet developing throughout the 1940s, affected the growth of an anti-romantic, anti-1940s movement. The importance of Philip Larkin's first meetings with Kingsley Amis, the St John's contemporary to whom he dedicated his *XX Poems* a decade later, has been well-documented. From 1944 to 1947 Larkin and Amis occasionally visited Oxford, and it was there that they first met John Wain, who had come up to St John's in 1943. Wain referred to Amis, who had returned to take a post-war degree, as 'united' with him 'in homage to Larkin'.[7] The first triumvirate of what would come to be known as 'The Movement' would continue to pay tribute to each other with compliments and dedications just as poets of the 1930s had.

Schooled from the first at Oxford by the anti-modernist predilections of tutors such as Gavin Bone and C. S. Lewis, these poets were urged to value a native classical style. In addition, they were influenced by such devotees of order and tradition as F. W. Bateson. Bateson (who would write glowingly of Philip Larkin and Donald Davie as 'Auden's (and Empson's) Heirs' in his 1957 *Essay in Criticism*) 'actually managed to recreate the eighteenth century model of the small homogeneous audience'[8] that would become important as an element of the Movement aesthetic.

A growing desire among editors and critics for poetry of exact statement and precise form reinforced the Movement poets' conservative intellectual training at Oxford. Rejecting religious and neo-romantic poets such as Edith Sitwell, Vernon Watkins and David Gascoyne, classically-oriented critics like Geoffrey Grigson renewed interest in Augustan poetry that the Movement was learning to revere. In his anthology *Before the Romantics* (1946), Grigson recommended reading poets of the eighteenth century to neutralize the bad effects of a 'colony of inky-cap toadstools' that he saw currently liquefying 'into a black neo-romantic mixture'.[9]

Confirmed in their anti-romanticism, Amis, Larkin and Wain found the first of several forums for their poetry in the Oxford magazine *Mandrake*. Edited in 1945–7 by Wain himself and Arthur Boyars, and later by Boyars alone or with co-editors, the little magazine offered an arena for the Movement to refine its aims and style. In the first stanza of Larkin's 'Portrait', published in *Mandrake I* (1946), we can already see the economy of statement that would become a prominent feature of the Movement style:

> Her hands intend no harm;
> Her hands devote themselves
> To sheltering a flame;
> Winds are her enemies,
> And everything that strives
> To bring her cold and darkness.

In 'Plymouth', published in the same issue, Larkin writes of his own development from lush romanticism to a more realistic style. The first two stanzas owe much to romantic verse; yet in the final stanza Larkin bows to Yeats as he moves away from the great master's sphere of influence:

> The hands that chose them rust upon a stick.
> Let my hands find such symbols, that can be
> Unnoticed in the casual light of day,
> Lying in wait for half a century
> To split chance lives across, that had not dreamed
> Such coast had echoed or such seabirds screamed.

In their contributions, Wain and Amis charted the restricted emotional field that would become a hallmark of early fifties poetry. Childhood is contrasted to the 'darkened room' of age; 'the black knight of living' calls the moves and 'our dreams no longer qualify us for / Returns to feeling of a life begun' ('Poem for Hilary' and 'Retrospect' by Amis, *Mandrake* I, 1947). The impermanent present offers only two safe actions in John Wain's 'The Last Time': to run away or die:

> And if, as we suspect, it is our fate
> To find that what we lost was always more,
> So that the ledger never works out straight

And each day finds us poorer than before;
Still it is searching makes us seem sublime,
Hoping each night to gain the happy shore,

To say for the last time there 'the last time'

Using an opportunity in 1949 to edit *Oxford Poetry* with James
Michie, Kingsley Amis further promoted what would become the
Movement style and tone. It is not surprising that the co-editors
traced a number of contributions back to the direct and
technically-controlled style of Auden. Although the Movement
would change their minds about Auden's importance, they were
willing to honour him in the late forties because he did not indulge
in the neo-romantic slush they saw all around them.

Elizabeth Jennings' 'Modern Poet', from *Oxford Poetry 1949*,
calls out for a new style:

This is no moment now for the fine phrases
The inflated sentence, words cunningly spun,
For the floreate image or the relaxing pun

. . .

And the poet's art is to speak and not to be sung
And sympathy must turn away to anger.

In 'Time' she anticipated Larkin's reliance on the present and
shared his despairing attitude toward a lost past and a grim
future:

Why cannot we accept the hour,
The present, be observers and
Hold a full knowledge in our power,
Arrest the falling of the sand?
And keep the watchful moment, pour
Its meaning in the hurried hand?

Probably Jennings had not met Larkin or Wain, but she knew
Amis in 1947 or 1948, and by the end of her studies at St Anne's,
she was aware of an emerging spare style among some poets at
Oxford.

In addition to the all-British nucleus at Oxford, a group of
talented Americans flourished during the early fifties there – and

these acquaintances of the Movement poets may well have contributed to the emphasis on formal qualities in poetry. In 1951, Donald Hall, a Harvard graduate who had edited the *Advocate* and studied under Richard Wilbur, enrolled at Christ Church. Along with Adrienne Rich, who brought Robert Lowell's early poetry of clarity to Oxford, Hall was able to influence British poetry during a transitional period. He edited the little magazine *New Poems* through six numbers and found the dominant tone to be the uneasiness that Fraser would note in the poetry of Thom Gunn two years later (Introduction to *Springtime*). Hall's own poem 'Exile' won the Newdigate prize in 1952. With a subject common to Oxford poets, the loss of childhood unity and an uncertainty about the present, Hall's major interest was formal. Like Wain, who later recalled using the strictest properties of verse to 'build' a system in time of ruin, Hall perceived reality in 1953 as a 'terrifying chaos outside form glimpsed only occasionally and never, of course, understood without translation into form'.[10] For Hall there was a distinct relationship between carefully structured poetry and the terror of a reality needing to be tamed.

At least one Movement poet had expressed needs and despairs similar to Hall's a decade earlier. Lines from Hall's 'Epithalamion' thematically gloss the first stanza of Philip Larkin's earliest published poem, the Audenesque 'Ultimatum' (*The Listener*, 28 November 1940).

> It is by choice and form
> We build defences from the storm.
> Imposed upon vacuities of space.
>
> (Hall)

> But we must build our walls, for what we are
> Necessitates it, and we must construct
> The ship to navigate behind them, there,
> Hopeless to ignore, helpless instruct
> For any term of time beyond the years
> That warn us of the need for emigration:
> Exploded the ancient saying: Life is yours.
>
> (Larkin)

Hall wrote of aesthetic walls and Larkin of walls against excesses of feeling. Yet by the early fifties the two sorts of walls had become one in combatting the lush excesses of neo-romanticism that threatened the Movement poets. The Movement poets were united by a desire to be completely honest in their feelings and responses; however the only way to achieve such honesty, they felt, was to control emotions.

Donald Davie, a Cambridge graduate who would become a contributor to the Movement anthologies in 1955–6, lent intellectual force to the platform with an emphasis on formal restraint. When in the November 1950 issue of *Poetry* (*London*) he commented on an anthology edited by Yvor Winters, he also spoke out to the new poets of the fifties: 'For the young English poet resentful of the tyranny of the "image" in the restricted sense of "metaphor" (whether inflated into symbols, worried into conceits, or compressed into "striking" epithets), this American anthology points to a direction which may provide a wholesome alternative, i.e., it points to a renewed poetry of statement, openly didactic but saved by a sedulously noble diction, from prosiness'.[11] In the early fifties, Davie, who had eagerly turned to Eliot's 'classicist' criticism during the forties,[12] viewed his own critical work *Purity of Diction in English Verse* (1952) as a manifesto for the new trend in poetry.

II POETRY IN THE WELFARE STATE: SOCIAL ORIGINS OF THE MOVEMENT

Poets of the small calm gesture, the controlled temper and the select academic audience, the Movement poets were apolitical, atheistic or agnostic, and mostly lower middle-class. Their aims and values cannot be easily divorced from the cultural and social milieu in which they grew up, the war and the early years of the Welfare State.

The war and its reconstruction era brought a change in the climate for poetry. Though the finest war poets were dead, except for Roy Fuller, many of the other 1940s poets such as Dylan Thomas were still writing. The British public, however, was more concerned now with immediate social tasks (new housing, jobs and rebuilding the nation) than with poetry. Consequently, poets who had not already forged reputations had a hard time catching the public eye – publishers considered the newcomers as risks.

The younger poets of the 1950s were left to their own devices to get published where and when they could. Many poets like Larkin and Amis were introduced by small presses (first in pamphlet form). In Oxford the painter-printer Oscar Mellor published Kingsley Amis, Donald Davie, Thom Gunn, John Holloway, Elizabeth Jennings, Philip Larkin and John Wain among others in a poetry series at his Fantasy Press. R. A. Caton, who had hoarded paper during the war, published Kingsley Amis' *Bright November* and built up a poetry list that included five Movement poets under the imprint of the Fortune Press. The Hand and Flower Press of Kent produced collections by Charles Causley, Michael Hamburger and Thomas Blackburn. The Marvell Press in Hull issued more of Larkin's work; Amis and Wain found a ready publisher in the Fine Art Department at Reading.

Throughout the social changes in the later forties and early fifties, a nagging feeling surfaced that poetry should have developed more radically than it had. In fact, social innovations seemed to have outdistanced art. Until the advent of the Movement platform in 1954 and the anthologies *Poets of the 1950s* (1955) and *New Lines* (1956), there was neither a major influential figure in modern poetry nor a new movement. The main trends of the war years, apart from war poetry, continued side by side: neo-romanticism, religious and metaphysical poetry, and some regional poetry. Not sure what would sell in 1945–6, editors such as those of *Orion*, Rosamond Lehmann, Edwin Muir, Denys Kilham Roberts and C. Day Lewis, opened the door to almost anything as long as it had what they called 'character'; old, new, traditional or experimental. In their first 1945 issue, they published an interview with Ivy Compton-Burnett, translations of Pasternak and Kafka, an article on Gustave Courbet, and 1931–2 poems by John Lehmann.

By the turn of the fifties, Alan Ross, who reviewed poetry for *The Listener*, confessed a despair among intellectuals. He pinpointed its source with words similar to those Charles Tomlinson would later use to criticize the Movement style emerging from this era: 'Failure of nerve'. 'The contemporary listlessness', explained Ross 'is the result of a succession of disillusions: political, scientific, moral. Against them religion and humanism have, up till now, proven ineffectual bulwarks. The future seems to be out of the hands of individuals.'[13] There were threats that seemed even worse than the horrors of war. Roy Fuller spelled out a terror about survival in peacetime in his 'Epitaphs for Soldiers':

Incredibly I lasted out a war,
Survived the unnatural, enormous danger
Of each enormous day. And so befell
A peril more enormous and still stranger:
The death by nature, chanceless, credible.

Such disillusionment was bred into the Movement poets, many of whom had served in the war before taking academic or administrative jobs.

Reviewing the post-war period of social change a decade later, G. S. Fraser determined that a lack of external event had created the artistic crisis. 'We had to revise our notions', he said. The poem was no longer a 'social product' as it had been during the 1930s or a 'psychological document' as it had been during the war years.[14] By 1953, Fraser and Iain Fletcher, who edited the poetry anthology *Springtime*, felt that they could detect a real difference in poetry. They acutely identified the newest literary ideals as a decorous tone, a chastely austere diction, and a stoical attitude complemented by a 'lack of sensuous richness'. Explaining Thom Gunn's work, Fraser and Fletcher isolated a current subject: 'In the most intimate of human relationships the poet is left with all the essential barriers still standing. He does not get out of himself, and that is what the poem is about; it leaves us feeling uneasy and unsatisfied, and it is also the significant contemporary theme'.[15] The very uneasiness that was felt socially and by those editing poetry in the late 1940s had become a poetic theme.

What occurred in poetry was not an isolated instance; Julian Symons has analyzed a similar change in detective fiction. Post-war crime writers approached the world differently from 1930s writers: 'Behind the detective stories written before the war there was a belief that human affairs could be ruled by reason and that virtue, generally identified with the established order of society, must prevail in the end'.[16] Readers aware of Nazi power, concentration camps and atomic bombs were no longer so easily 'deceived' (the word is Symons') by puzzling murder plots that could be solved by a logician's reasoning powers. Instead, crime writers now chose to stress the vagaries of human character and the capriciousness of human motive.

The Movement's two chief reactions to wartime and post-war Britain – resignation and a desire to carve out some small amount of happiness – became part of a total literary style.[17] When the

Movement poets recalled their own early lives, they stressed feelings of uncertainty and the sense of being hemmed in by circumstances. Born in the span of years 1917–30, the Movement poets were in their twenties or early thirties in 1950. Some had grown up during the years of the depression and the Spanish Civil War, and had reached university or a first job on the eve of the war. John Wain poignantly confided what other poets of his generation may also have felt: 'From the beginning I saw the world as something to be feared'.[18] Larkin recalled the claustrophobic atmosphere of reaching manhood in the early 1940s: 'At an age when self-importance would have been normal, events cut us ruthlessly down to size'.[19] Even Thom Gunn, who was evacuated from London as a child during the Blitz, associated his youth with a loss of something unnameable though yearned for. His poem from the 1970s, 'Autobiography', captures the elegiac feelings that attended his childhood:

> . . .
> life seemed all
> loss, and what was more
> I'd lost whatever it was
> before I'd even had it

Assuming that to write about external events would only recreate a fragmentation they already felt, the Movement poets preferred to devote themselves to elegies or self-reflexive poetry. Their hostility to the Apocalyptics, those doyens of incoherence, is more understandable given their own desperate need for order. In Elizabeth Jennings' words: the Movement poets' work was a 'passionately intelligent gesture against chaos'.[20] John Wain more specifically defined the nature of that gesture: poets felt 'the impulse to build . . . to make something among the ruins. Writing in regular and disciplined verse forms is building in a simple and obvious sense.'[21]

III FALSE CLAIMS FOR THE MOVEMENT: THEIR HERITAGE IN THE 1940S

During the years 1953–6, publicity for the Movement poets increased until they were heralded as the 'new' group in poetry. In

spite of the fact that they appeared to have strikingly fresh ideas
about poetry, they were not united in their values and practices,
nor were they completely different from poets in the decade before
them. In fact, certain preoccupations and attitudes from the 1940s
were automatically absorbed by the Movement.

On 27 August 1954, Anthony Hartley wrote a leading article for
The Spectator on new 'Poets of the Fifties'. There he drew a portrait
of a group of poets who, united by a 'zeitgeist', found their roots in
the poetry of the 1930s; they were anti-romantic and anti-
modernist. English poetry, he avowed, had been 'ravaged by the
indiscriminate use of evocatory images' during the decade before.
The 1940s poets had been bardic windbags; these new poets, on
the other hand, were witty, clever, ironic, and fond of complexity
and ambiguity. Far more than the 1940s, they attempted to
convey 'complicated thought and moral feeling'.[22]

On 1 October 1954, a mere six weeks later, 'In the Movement'
(an anonymous article written by the literary editor J. D. Scott),
was published in *The Spectator*. It is well known that this piece of
persuasive journalism awarded the Movement its name and
defined its mission. Though Scott described the writers as
'incohesive', he predicted that their style would carry the day into
the sixties and seventies. These two *Spectator* articles attracted
attention for two reasons: Hartley and Scott were the first to
provide a name and a platform for the Movement, and their
superior and decisive tone shocked much of the literary world into
believing them.

Suggesting that the world had indeed changed, *The Spectator*
announced the arrival of the long-awaited new literary generation:

> The Movement, as well as being anti-phoney, is anti-wet;
> sceptical, robust, ironic, prepared to be as comfortable as
> possible in a wicked, commercial, threatened world which
> doesn't look, anyway, as if it's going to be changed much by
> handfuls of young English writers.[23]

Identifying the members of the Movement as Kingsley Amis,
Donald Davie, Thom Gunn, Iris Murdoch and John Wain, Scott
delivered the group of prose and poetry writers to an audience
who, he implied, had been suffering ever since Auden had sailed
to America and other 1930s poets disbanded. 'Whatever young

writers did in the post-war years, they did it individually,' he proclaimed, 'whatever excitement there was, it was communal.'

While some intellectuals were sceptical that a movement existed or was even needed, two poetry anthologies, *Poets of the 1950s* (1955) edited by D. J. Enright, and *New Lines* (1956) edited by Robert Conquest, attempted to silence naysayers. Misreading the moral intentions of the Romanticism of the 1940s and 'treading down' the forties generally, Enright implied that faith in mankind was now foolish. The new poet's job was 'not to whitewash but to get beneath the mud; and this necessitates not only a willingness to recognize the virtues when and where they are met with, but also a fairly tough intelligence and an unwillingness to be deceived'. The Movement might surprise the literary world but it would brook no surprises itself. The contributors to Enright's volume – Kingsley Amis, Elizabeth Jennings, Robert Conquest, Donald Davie, John Holloway, Philip Larkin and John Wain – did not have as much in common as Enright claimed, yet they realized the publicity value of a group identity.

Along with *The Spectator*, *Poets of the 1950s* paved the way for *New Lines*. As Howard Sergeant has remarked,[24] few anthologies in the history of literature can have had as much advance publicity as *New Lines* did. At the time and ever since it was published in 1956, the Movement has been chastised because of an overt publicity campaign. Retaining Enright's crew, Conquest added one poet to his anthology, Thom Gunn, and stated the goal of the group in terms which recall T. S. Eliot's prescriptions for the public good. He saw the Movement's mission as one of changing the public taste by correcting a prevailing mood. The introduction to *New Lines* also recalls a manifesto congenial to Eliot – Hulme's 'Romanticism and Classicism' (1913–14) first published in 1924 and reprinted in 1936 and 1949. Both Conquest and Hulme called for a 'dry, hard' poetic style.[25] Both resisted what Conquest called an unhealthy modern taste for 'diffuse and sentimental verbiage', 'hollow technical pirouettes', and a 'surrender' to subjectivity.[26]

There were, unquestionably, several significant discrepancies in the programmes: a *TLS* reviewer of *Poets of the 1950s* and *New Lines* was prompt to notice such differences: 'certainly the range of styles, of tones, in these anthologies is much more various than recent polemics about the "new movement" might have led the ordinary reader to expect' (13 July 1956).

One of the most misleading statements made about the Movement poets implied that they were radically new. Conquest claimed that their empiricism and their ability to concentrate on the 'real person or event' marked them off from their predecessors. Unlike the poets of the 1940s, they 'refused to abandon a rational structure and comprehensible language'. With the aesthetics of clarity and form, the Movement appeared to have no tie with the previous decade.

Yet the 1940s and 1950s shared certain attitudes, styles and subjects. Indeed the ideals of the Movement that were touted as so new – clarity and lucidity – were already amply evident in the best poetry of the 1940s. In addition, frustration at 'undone years' lies behind much of the poetry of both the 1940s and early 1950s.

In the war decade's topographical poetry of exile, the 1950s poets discovered a strong sense of place. Yet of the two examples below, it is paradoxically the first, published in 1956, which is the more lush and exotic.

> Nothing by halves. This richness is a passion that
>   never rests
> From ripeness moved to raging, from the knotted
>   rosebud to the scattered leaves.
> Proud mountain, luminous citron, azure coast –
>   they do not grow
> Without the shrivelling thunderbolt, the tired
>   and flaking walls.
>
> ('Baie des Anges, Nice', D. J. Enright)

The second example, though written in exile during the war, travels easily between two decades. It is simple, detailed, and more overtly addresses the relationship between the intellect and its object:

> The simple beach and the sea. And separate things
> lie on this openness as on a hand;
> sea-colored tents, a boat upon its side
> Scarlet of flags, a children's see-saw, swings,
> like elementary shapes a child has drawn;
> and the mind grasps them in a stride.
>
> ('The Ship', Bernard Spencer)

If we look for clarity and bareness of figurative language in the forties, Alun Lewis can suffice to match a Wain or Davie. The last stanza from 'Raiders' Dawn' (1941) sounds more Augustan than many Movement lines:

> Blue necklace left
> On a charred chair
> Tells that beauty
> Was startled there.

Amis' 'Masters' has a stricter syllable count and is more finished than Lewis' similarly aphoristic 'Shadows'. Still, though Lewis tries to render a wavering indecision, he nonetheless equals Amis' thoughtful compression:

> By yielding mastery the will is freed,
> For it is by surrender that we live,
> And we are taken if we wish to give,
>   Are needed if we need.
>
> (Amis)

> He chooses best who does not choose
> Time and all its lies;
> He who makes the end and the beginning one
> Within himself grows wise.
>
> (Lewis)

The donnish and rational poetry of the Movement was known for a precisely hewn irony. Often self-directed, irony functioned as an element through which the poet could set forth his ambiguous attitudes towards life without ever being deceived. Yet if irony is a hallmark of the 1950s poets, then Roy Fuller can be invoked as a poet from the 1940s who is every bit as humorous at his own expense as Larkin. Conversely, Drummond Allison's wry summation 'Epitaph', a poem undated but probably written between 1941 and 1943, could easily have been composed in the 1950s: 'He at any rate knew the certainty / Of the second best's utility / He was the healthy but ugly baby / . . . The man who made fifty.'

If certain poets of the 1950s found detachment through dispassionate 'records' or 'observations' (Wain and Jennings, for instance), they followed a precedent set by Keith Douglas in

'Enfidaville'. Larkin's and Conquest's photography poems, which capture particular moments in time, were anticipated in poems such as Roy Fuller's 'The Middle of a War' and 'The Photographs'. In spite of major differences between poetry of the 1940s and the early 1950s, a look at such similarities shows that the 'new' poets of the fifties had a rich heritage in the decade before them.

Perhaps even more important, at least five Movement poets – Kingsley Amis, Donald Davie, D. J. Enright, Philip Larkin and John Wain – were born into the same generation as the prominent war-poets. They grew up during cultural crisis; they shared early preoccupations with a life aborted and devalued by the spectre of death. While separated from colleagues by their ultimate linguistic strategies in poetry and their reliance on language as substance, their dismissal of the 1940s poets seems more than a simple, ritualistic Oedipal impulse. Rather, their dissociation is yet another self-protective gesture against an overwhelming chaos that we still face today, a chaos that the best poets of the 1940s did not flinch from confronting directly.

NOTES

1. Philip Larkin, *The North Ship* (London: Faber & Faber, 1966) p. 9.
2. John Wain, 'Ambiguous Gifts', *Penguin New Writing* (40), 1950, p. 127.
3. Blake Morrison, *The Movement* (Oxford: Oxford University Press, 1980) p. 25.
4. Philip Larkin, 'The War Poet', *The Listener* (10 October 1963) pp. 561–2. For a similar compliment to Owen at the expense of the 1940s war poets, see D. J. Enright, *The Poets of the 1950s*, preface (Tokyo: Kenkyusha Ltd., 1955) p. 8.
5. William Butler Yeats, introduction, *The Oxford Book of Modern Verse 1892–1935* (Oxford: The Clarendon Press, 1936) pp. xxxiv–xxxv.
6. Larkin, 'The War Poet', p. 562.
7. John Wain, *Sprightly Running* (London: Macmillan, 1962) pp. 187–8.
8. Morrison, *The Movement*, p. 116.
9. Geoffrey Grigson, *Before the Romantics* (London: Routledge, 1946) pp. vii–viii. Also see Geoffrey Grigson, 'The Language of Poetry', and 'The Enjoyment of Poetry', *Essays from the Air* (London: 1951) pp. 171–7. Grigson proposes Hardy as a 'sad' but 'honest' poet who might be a good model to counter neo-romanticism.
10. Donald Hall, quoted by Eric Homberger, *The Art of the Real* (London: Dent, 1977) p. 87.
11. Donald Davie, 'The Spoken Word', reprinted in *The Poet in the Imaginary Museum* (Manchester: Carcanet Press, 1977) p. 5.

12. Donald Davie, 'Eliot in One Poet's Life', *Mosaic* 6 (Fall 1972) pp. 229–41. Also, letter to the author, 20 June 1980.
13. Alan Ross, 'English Poetry Today', *The Listener*, XLIII (25 May 1950) p. 923.
14. G. S. Fraser, 'The Poet and His Medium', in John Lehmann (ed.), *The Craft of Letters* (London: The Cresset Press, 1956) p. 113.
15. G. S. Fraser and Iain Fletcher (eds), *Springtime* (London: Peter Owen Limited, 1953) pp. 7–12.
16. Julian Symons, *The Detective Story in Britain* (London: Longman, 1962) pp. 34–5.
17. Eric Homberger, *The Art of the Real* (London: Dent, 1977) p. 74.
18. Wain, *Sprightly Running*, p. 58.
19. Philip Larkin, *Jill* (New York: The Woodstock Press, 1976) Introduction.
20. Elizabeth Jennings (ed.), *An Anthology of Modern Verse* 1940–1960 (London: Methuen, 1961) p. 10.
21. John Wain (ed.), *An Anthology of Modern Poetry* (London: Hutchinson, 1963; 1967 edn) p. 35.
22. Anthony Hartley, 'Poets of the Fifties', *Spectator* (27 August 1954) p. 260.
23. Anon. (J. D. Scott), 'In the Movement', *Spectator* (1 October 1954) p. 400.
24. Howard Sergeant, 'The Movement – an Agreed Fiction?', in Dannie Abse (ed.), *Best Poetry of the Year 6* (London: Robson Books, 1979) pp. 127–8.
25. T. E. Hulme, 'Romanticism and Classicism', *Speculations* (London: Routledge & Kegan Paul, 1924; 1936; 1949). See especially pp. 126–7 and 133.
26. Robert Conquest (ed.), *New Lines* (London: Macmillan, 1956) pp. xii–xiv.

Bibliography

I PRIMARY SOURCES

Abse, Dannie and Howard Sergeant (eds), *Mavericks* (London: Editions Poetry and Poverty, 1957).

Allison, Drummond, *The Poems of Drummond Allison* (ed. Michael Sharp) (University of Reading Whiteknights Press, 1978; limited edition).

——, *The Yellow Night* (London: The Fortune Press, 1944).

Allott, Kenneth, introduction, *The Penguin Book of Contemporary Verse* (Harmondsworth: Penguin, 1950, reprinted 1978).

Alvarez, A. (ed.), *The New Poetry* (Harmondsworth: Penguin, 1962, revised 1966).

Amis, Kingsley, *A Case of Samples: Poems 1946–56* (London: Victor Gollancz, 1956).

——, 'Communication and the Victorian Poet', *Essays in Criticism*, IV, 4 (1954) pp. 386–9.

——, *A Frame of Mind: Eighteen Poems* (University of Reading Fine Art Department, 1953).

—— and James Michie (eds), *Oxford Poetry 1949* (Oxford: Basil Blackwell, 1949).

Auden, W. H., *Collected Poems* (ed. Edward Mendelson) (New York: Random House, 1976).

——, *Collected Shorter Poems 1930–1944* (London: Faber & Faber, 1950).

——, *The Dyer's Hand and other Essays* (New York: Random House, 1962).

——, *Selected Poems* (ed. Edward Mendelson) (New York: Random House, new edition, 1979).

——, 'T. E. Lawrence', *Now and Then*, 47 (Spring 1934) p. 30.

Bain, Donald, (ed.), *Oxford and Cambridge Writing* (Cambridge University Press, 1942).

Baker, Denys Val, (ed.), *Little Reviews Anthology 1914–1943* (London: George Allen and Unwin, 1943).

——, 'A Review of War Time Reviews' in Stefan Schimanski and Henry Treece (eds), *Transformation 3* (London: Victor Gollancz, 1945).

Bancroft, Ian, 'Review of Henry Treece's *Invitation and Warning*' *Poetry Quarterly*, IV (Summer 1942) pp. 76–8.

Barker, George, 'The Miracle of Images', *Orpheus*, 12 (1949) pp. 133–6.

Bateson, F. W., 'Auden's (and Empson's) Heirs', *Essays in Criticism*, VII (1957) pp. 76–80.

Bayliss, John and Nicholas Moore, Douglas Newton (eds), *The Fortune Anthology* (London: The Fortune Press, 1942).

Bell, William (ed.), *More Poetry from Oxford* (London: The Fortune Press, 1947).
——, *Poetry from Oxford in Wartime* (London: The Fortune Press, 1946).
Benn, Robert, and Dennis Birch, Robert Smith, Alan White (eds), *Poets in Battle Dress* (London: The Fortune Press, 1942).
Bergonzi, Bernard, Letter, *Spectator*, 3 September 1954, p. 280.
Blackburn, Thomas (ed.), *1945–1960, An Anthology of English Poetry* (London: Putnam, 1960).
Blythe, Ronald, (ed.), *Components of the Scene: Stories, Poems and Essays of the Second World War* (Harmondsworth: Penguin, 1966).
Bowen, Elizabeth, *The Heat of the Day* (London: Jonathan Cape, 1949; Harmondsworth: Penguin, 1962, reprinted, 1983; New York: Knopf, 1949).
——, *Ivy Gripped the Steps* (New York: Knopf, 1946).
Brooke, Rupert, *The Poetical Works of Rupert Brooke* (ed. Geoffrey Keynes) (London: Faber & Faber, 1946).
——, *The Letters of Rupert Brooke* (ed. Geoffrey Keynes) (London: Faber & Faber, 1968).
Brownjohn, Alan, Letter, *Spectator*, 8 October 1954, pp. 434–5.
Comfort, Alex, 'English Poetry and the War', *Partisan Review*, X, 2 (March 1943) pp. 191–3.
—— and Robert Graecen (eds), *Lyra: An Anthology of New Lyric* (Essex: Grey Walls Press, 1942).
Connolly, Cyril, *Enemies of Promise* (London: Routledge & Kegan Paul, first published 1938, revised 1949).
—— (pseudonym Palinurus), *The Unquiet Grave*. Written from a journal kept 1942–3. First published in *Horizon* in 1944; rev. Hamish Hamilton, 1945; introduction by author added 1951; London: Arrow Books, 1961, reprinted from the 1951 edition).
Currey, R. N. and G. V. Gibson (eds), *Poems from India* (London: Oxford University Press, 1945).
——, *Tiresias and Other Poems* (London: Oxford University Press, 1940).
Daiches, David, 'Contemporary Poetry in Britain', *Poetry (Chicago)*, LXII (1943) pp. 150–64.
Davie, Donald, *Collected Poems 1950–1970* (Oxford University Press, 1972).
——, introduction, *Purity of Diction in English Verse* (London: Chatto & Windus, 1952).
Deutch, Babette, 'War Poetry Then and Now', *New Republic*, CIV (21 April 1941) pp. 565–7.
Dobrée, Bonamy, 'English Poets Today: The Younger Generation', *Sewanee Review*, LXII, 4 (Autumn 1954) pp. 598–620.
Douglas, Keith, *Alamein to Zem Zem* (London: Editions Poetry London, 1946; reprinted Oxford University Press, 1966; 1979).
—— and Alec M. Hardie (eds), *Augury: An Oxford Miscellany of Prose and Verse* (Oxford: Basil Blackwell, 1940).
——, *The Collected Poems of Keith Douglas* (eds, G. S. Fraser, J. C. Hall, John Waller) (London: Editions Poetry London, 1951; reprinted Faber & Faber, 1966).
——, *Complete Poems of Keith Douglas* (ed. Desmond Graham) (London: Oxford University Press, 1979).

——, 'Poets in This War', Add. MS. 53773, reprinted in *TLS* (23 April 1971) p. 478.

——, *Selected Poems of Keith Douglas* (ed. Ted Hughes) (London: Faber & Faber, 1964).

Durrell, Lawrence, *Cities, Plains, and People* (London: Faber & Faber, 1946).

Eliot, T. S., 'Last Words', *The Criterion*, XVIII, 31 (January 1939) pp. 272–5.

Enright, D. J. (ed.), *Poets of the 1950s: An Anthology of New English Verse* (Tokyo: Kenkyusha Press, 1955).

——, 'Ruins and Warnings', Review of Henry Treece's *Invitation and Warning*, *Scrutiny*, XI (Summer 1942) pp. 78–80.

Ewart, Gavin, *Poems and Songs* (London: The Fortune Press, 1943).

Fausset, Hugh l'Anson, 'The Broken Arch', *TLS* (8 August 1942) p. 382.

——, 'The Innocent Eye', *TLS* (17 March 1945) p. 128.

——, 'To the Poets of 1940', *TLS* (30 December 1940) p. 755.

——, 'Three Poets', *TLS* (2 September 1944) p. 428.

——, 'Where Poetry Stands', *TLS* (6 September 1941) p. 450.

Fedden, Robin (ed.), *Personal Landscape, An Anthology of Exile* (London: Editions Poetry Ltd., 1945).

Fords and Bridges, J. C. Moore and Nicholas Moore (eds), V, 1939–40.

Forster, E. M., 'Books of the Year', *The Listener*, 23 (11 January 1940) p. 86.

Fraser, G. S., *Home Town Elegy* (London: Editions Poetry London, 1944).

——, *Leaves Without a Tree* (Japan: Hokuseido Press, 1953).

——, *Poems* (eds Iain Fletcher and John Lucas) (Leicester University Press, 1981).

——, 'A Poet of Rare Promise', *TLS* (26 April 1947) p. 198.

——, 'Recent Verse: London and Cairo', *Poetry (London)*, 10 (1945) pp. 217–19.

——, and Iain Fletcher (eds), *Springtime* (London: Peter Owen, 1953).

——, *A Stranger and Afraid* (Manchester: Carcanet Press, 1983).

——, *The Traveller Has Regrets* (London: The Harvill Press and Editions Poetry London, 1948).

Fuller, Roy, *Collected Poems 1936–61* (London: André Deutsch, 1962).

——, *Epitaphs and Occasions* (London: John Lehmann, 1949).

——, *A Lost Season* (London: The Hogarth Press, 1944).

——, *The Middle of a War* (London: The Hogarth Press, 1942).

——, *An Old War* (Edinburgh: The Tragara Press, 1974, limited edition).

——, *Poems* (London: The Fortune Press, 1940).

——, War Poems from 'An Old File', *The Listener*, 82 (4 December 1969) pp. 798–9.

Gardiner, Wrey, *The Dark Thorn* (An Autobiography) (London: The Grey Walls Press, 1946).

——, *The Flowering Moment* (Autobiographical Reminiscences) (London: The Grey Walls Press, 1949).

Gardner, Brian (ed.), *The Terrible Rain: The War Poets 1939–45* (London: Magnum Books, 1966; 1977).

Gascoyne, David, *Collected Poems* (ed. Robin Skelton) (London: Oxford University Press, 1965).

——, *A Short Survey of Surrealism* (London: Frank Cass 1970; first published 1935).

Grant, Douglas, 'War and the Writer', *Penguin Parade*, second series III (1948) pp. 57–68.

Graves, Robert, *Poems 1939–45* (London: Cassell, 1946).

——, 'War Poetry in this War', *The Listener*, 26 (23 October 1941) p. 566.

Grigson, Geoffrey, *Before the Romantics* (London: Routledge, 1946).

——, *Essays from the Air* (London: Routledge, 1951).

—— (ed.), *Poetry of the Present: An Anthology of the Thirties and After* (London: Phoenix House, 1949).

——, 'Twenty-Seven Sonnets', *New Verse*, NS I, 2 (May 1939) p. 49.

Hall, Donald, *Exile* (Newdigate Prize Poem) (Oxford: Fantasy Press, 1952).

Hamilton, Ian (ed.), *The Poetry of War 1939–45* (London: Alan Ross, 1965).

Hartley, Anthony, 'Poets of the Fifties', *Spectator* (27 August 1954) pp. 260–1.

Hawkins, Desmond, 'Interview' with Cyril Connolly *The Listener* (5 December 1940) p. 812.

Heath-Stubbs, John, *Beauty and the Beast* (London: Routledge, 1943).

——, *The Charity of the Stars* (New York: William Sloane Associates, 1949).

—— and David Wright (eds), *The Faber Book of Twentieth-Century Verse* (London: Faber & Faber, 1953).

—— (ed.), *Images of Tomorrow: An Anthology* (London: SCM Press, 1953).

——, Personal interview with G. H. B. Wightman. *Aquarius* 10 (1978) pp. 72–90.

——, *Wounded Thammuz* (London: Routledge, 1942).

Henderson, Hamish, *Elegies for the Dead in Cyrenaica* (London: John Lehmann, 1948).

Hendry, J. F. and Henry Treece (eds), *The Crown and the Sickle* (London: P. S. King and Staples, 1944).

—— and others (eds), *The New Apocalypse* (London: The Fortune Press, 1941).

——, 'The Philosophy of Herbert Read', in Henry Treece (ed.), *Herbert Read* (London: Faber & Faber, 1945).

—— (ed.), *The White Horseman* (London: Routledge, 1941).

Hillary, Richard, *The Last Enemy* (London: Macmillan, 1942).

Horizon (ed. Cyril Connolly), volumes 1–20 (London 1940–50).

Jennings, Elizabeth (ed.), *An Anthology of Modern Verse* 1940–1960 (London: Methuen, 1961).

——, *Poetry To-Day, 1957–60* (New York: Longman, 1960).

Jones, Gwyn, 'Alun Lewis', *The Welsh Review*, III, 2 (June 1944) pp. 118–21.

Jones, Phyllis (ed.), *Modern Verse 1900–1940* (Oxford University Press, 1940).

Keyes, Sidney, and Michael Meyer (eds), *Eight Oxford Poets* (London: Routledge, 1941).

——, *Minos of Crete* (ed. Michael Meyer) (London: Routledge, 1948).

——, *The Collected Poems of Sidney Keyes* (ed. Michael Meyer) (London: Routledge, 1945; 1946).

Khaki and Blue (ed. Peter Ratazzi) (London: 1–5, 1944–5).

Kingdom Come (ed. John Waller) (Oxford: 1–3, 1939–1940).

Larkin, Philip, *All What Jazz: A Record Diary 1961–1968* (London: Faber & Faber, 1970; New York: St. Martin's Press, 1970).

——, *High Windows* (London: Faber & Faber, 1974; New York: Farrar, Strauss & Giroux, 1974).

——, *Jill* (London: The Fortune Press, 1946; 2nd edn, introduced by Philip

Larkin, London: Faber & Faber 1964; 1st paperback edn; Faber & Faber 197*[*
Woodstock, New York; The Overlook Press, 1976).
——, *The Less Deceived* (London: The Marvell Press, 1955).
——, *The North Ship* (London: The Fortune Press, 1945; 2nd edn, introduced by
Philip Larkin with an additional poem taken from *XX Poems*, London and
Boston, Massachusetts: Faber & Faber, 1966).
——, introduction, *The Oxford Book of Twentieth-Century English Verse*, edited by
Philip Larkin (Oxford: The Clarendon Press, 1973).
——, *Poems* (Eynsham: Fantasy Press, 1954. No. 21 in the Fantasy Poets series).
——, *XX Poems* (Belfast: privately printed, 1951).
——, 'Wanted Good Hardy Critic', *Critical Quarterly*, 8, 2 (Summer 1966)
pp. 174–9.
——, 'The War Poet', *The Listener* (10 October 1963) pp. 561–2.
——, *The Whitsun Weddings* (London and Boston, Massachusetts: Faber & Faber,
1964).
Ledward, Patricia and Colin Strang (eds), *Poems from this War* (Cambridge
University Press, 1942).
Lehmann, John, 'A Human Standpoint' on Alun Lewis, in his *The Open Night*
(New York: Harcourt Brace, 1952).
——, *I Am My Brother* (Autobiography volume II) (London: Longman, 1960).
——, *The Whispering Gallery* (Autobiography volume I) (London: Longman,
1955).
Lehmann, Rosamond, and Edwin Muir, Denys Kilham Roberts, and C. Day
Lewis (eds), *Orion, a Miscellany* (London: Nicholson and Watson, 1945).
Lewis, Alun, *Ha! Ha! Among the Trumpets* (London: George Allen and Unwin,
1945).
——, *In the Green Tree* (London: George Allen and Unwin, 1948).
——, *The Last Inspection* (New York: Macmillan, 1943).
——, *Letters from India* (Cardiff: Penmark Press, 1946).
——, *Raiders' Dawn* (New York: Macmillan, 1942).
——, *Selected Poetry and Prose* (ed. Ian Hamilton) (London: George Allen and
Unwin, 1966).
Listen Hessle: I, 1954–5.
The Listener, volumes 23–42, 1940–49.
Lucas, F. L., *Journey Under the Terror* (London: Cassell, 1939).
Lucie-Smith, Edward (ed.), *British Poetry Since 1945, An Anthology* (Harmonds-
worth: Penguin, 1970).
MacNiece, Louis, 'Lost Generations?', review of *Poetry Now* and *Mavericks*, *London
Magazine* 4, 4 (April 1957) pp. 42–55.
Manning, Olivia, 'Poets in Exile', *Horizon* (October 1944) pp. 270–9.
Matthews, William (ed.), *British Diaries 1442–1942* (Berkeley: University of
California Press, 1950).
Meyer, Michael, 'Sidney Keyes: A Memoir', *The Windmill*, I (1944) p. 57.
Modern Reading (ed. Reginald Moore) (London: 7,8, 1943–4).
Moore, Geoffrey (ed.), *Poetry from Cambridge in Wartime* (London: The Fortune
Press, 1946).
Moore, Nicholas, *Recollections of the Gala*, *Selected Poems 1943–48* (London: Editions
Poetry London, 1950).
The New Apocalypse, The Fortune Press, 1938.

New Writing (ed. John Lehmann) Nos. 1–3, 1938–9.

New Writing and Daylight (ed. John Lehmann) irregular, 1943–1946.

Nicholson, Norman (ed.), *An Anthology of Religious Verse Designed for the Times* (Harmondsworth: Penguin, 1942).

——, *Man and Literature* (London: SCM Press, 1943).

Nine (eds Peter Russell, G. S. Fraser, Iain Fletcher) I, 1–5 (1949–50).

Orwell, George, *The Collected Essays, Journalism and Letters*, I–IV (New York: Harvest Books, 1968).

——, 'English Writing in Total War', *New Republic*, CV (14 July 1941) pp. 57–8.

——, Review of *The New Apocalypse*, *Life and Letters To-Day*, XXV (June 1940) pp. 315–18.

Owen, Wilfred, *The Collected Poems of Wilfred Owen* (ed. C. Day Lewis) (New York: New Directions, 1963).

Our Time (eds Beatrix Lehmann, John Banting, Ben Frankel, Randall Swingler) I, 1941.

Outposts (ed. Howard Sergeant) 1–4, 1944.

Penguin New Writing (ed. John Lehmann) (Harmondsworth: volumes 1–40, 1941–50).

Personal Landscape (eds Robin Fedden *et al.*,) Cairo: 1–8, 1942–45.

Peschman, H., *The Voice of Poetry (1930–1950)*, *An Anthology* (London: Evans, 1950; rep. 1969).

Poetry (London) (ed. Tambimuttu) I and II; 1–10, 12, 14, 15, 1939–49.

Poetry Quarterly (ed. Wrey Gardiner) 1939–1953.

'Poets of Moderation', (Anon.) Review of *New Lines* and *Poets of the 1950s*, *TLS* (13 July 1956) p. 424.

Poets of Tomorrow, series 1–3 (London: The Hogarth Press, 1939–42).

Prince, F. T., *Collected Poems* (London: Anvil Press Poetry, 1979; and New York: The Sheep Meadow Press, 1979).

Pudney, John and Henry Treece (eds), *Air Force Poetry* (London: Bodley Head, 1944).

Read, Sir Herbert, *Form in Modern Poetry* (London: Vision Press, 1948, first printing 1932).

——, *The Meaning of Art* (London: Faber & Faber, 1931; 3rd ed. 1951).

——, 'The New Romantic School', *The Listener* (23 April 1942) pp. 533–4.

——, *Poetry and Anarchism* (London: Faber & Faber, 1938).

——, *Selected Writings of Herbert Read* (foreword Allen Tate) (London: Faber & Faber, 1963).

——, *Surrealism* (London: Faber & Faber, 1936; imprint varies).

Reed, Henry, 'Poetry in War Time: The Younger Poets', *The Listener* (25 January 1945) pp. 100–1.

Rhys, Kiedrych (ed.), *Poems from the Forces* (London: Routledge, 1941).

Ridler, Anne (ed.), *A Little Book of Modern Verse* (preface T. S. Eliot) (London: Faber & Faber, 1946).

Ross, Alan, 'English Poetry Today', *The Listener*, XLIII (25 May 1950) pp. 923–4.

——, *The Forties* (London: The Haycock Press, 1950).

——, *Poetry 1945–50* (New York: Longman, 1951).

Ross, Julian Maclaren, *Memoirs of the Forties* (London: Alan Ross, 1965).

——, 'Second Lieutenant Alun Lewis', *Penguin New Writing*, 27 (April 1946) pp. 78–80.

Savage, D. S., *The Personal Principle: Studies in Modern Poetry* (London: Routledge, 1944).

Scarfe, Francis, *Auden and After* (London: Routledge, 1942).

Schimanski, Stefan, and Henry Treece, *Leaves in the Storm: A Book of Diaries with Running Commentary* (London: Lindsay Drummond, 1947).

——, *A New Romantic Anthology* (London: Grey Walls Press, 1949).

——, *Transformation* (London: Victor Gollancz, 1943, 1945).

——, *Wartime Harvest* (London: J. Bale and Staples, 1943).

Scott, J. D. (Anon.) 'In the Movement', *Spectator*, 193 (1 October 1954) pp. 399–400.

Sergeant, Howard (ed.), *For Those Who Are Alive* (London: The Fortune Press, 1946).

——, *These Years* (Leeds: E. J. Arnold and Sons, 1950).

——, 'A Time for Decision', *Khaki and Blue* (1945), 59.

——, 'Tradition in the Making of Modern Poetry (London: Britannicus Liber, 1951).

Silkin, Jon, *The Penguin Book of First World War Poetry* (Harmondsworth: Penguin, 1979).

Singer, John, Review of *The Crown and the Sickle*, *Poetry Quarterly*, VII (Spring 1945) p. 37–9.

Skelton, Robin (ed.) *Poetry of the Forties* (Harmondsworth: Penguin, 1968).

Spencer, Bernard, *Aegean Islands and Other Poems* (London: Editions Poetry London, 1946).

——, *Collected Poems* (London: Alan Ross, 1965).

——, *Collected Poems* (ed. Roger Bowen) (London: Oxford University Press, 1981).

——, Personal interview with Peter Orr, *The Poet Speaks* (London: Routledge & Kegan Paul, 1966).

Spender, Stephen, 'The Influence of Rilke on English Poetry', *The Listener*, 36 (18 July 1946) pp. 84–5.

——, *The New Realism* (London: The Hogarth Press, 1939).

——, 'On Literary Movements', *Encounter*, I, 2 (November 1953) pp. 66–8.

——, 'Poetry for Poetry's Sake and Poetry Beyond Poetry', *Horizon*, XIII (April 1946) pp. 221–38.

——, 'Poetry in 1941', *Horizon*, V (February 1942) pp. 96–111.

——, *Poetry Since 1939* (London: Longman, 1946).

——, 'Rilke's Letters to this War', *The New Statesman and Nation*, XX (6 July 1940) pp. 10–11.

——, 'September Journal', *Horizon*, I, 2, 3, 5 (February, March, May 1940) pp. 103–21; 211–22; 356–63.

——, 'War and the Writer', *Partisan Review*, IX, 1 (January/February 1942) pp. 63–6.

——, *World within World* (London: Hamish Hamilton, 1951).

——, 'The Year's Poetry, 1940', *Horizon*, III, (February 1940) pp. 138–48.

Stanford, Derek, 'The Black Seasons', *Poetry Quarterly*, VII (Spring 1945) pp. 29–30.

——, *Dylan Thomas* (London: Neville Spearman, 1954).

——, *The Freedom of Poetry* (London: Falcon Press, 1947).

——, *Inside the Forties: Literary Memoirs 1937–1957* (London: Sidgwick & Jackson, 1977).

Stavely, Tom, 'The Boyhood of a Poet', *The Listener*, 37 (23 January 1947) pp. 162–3.

Stonier, G. W., 'Poetry and the War', *The New Statesman and Nation*, XXVIII (2 September 1944) p. 155.

Symons, Julian, *Notes from Another Country* (memoirs) (London: London Magazine Editions, 1972).

Tambimuttu (ed.), *Poetry in Wartime* (London: Faber & Faber, 1942).

Thomas, Dylan, *Collected Poems 1934–1952* (London: Dent, 1952).

——, *The Map of Love* (London: Dent, 1939).

——, *Selected Letters of Dylan Thomas* (ed. Constantine Fitzgibbon) (London: Dent, 1966).

Thwaite, Anthony, Letter, *Spectator* (8 October 1954) p. 434.

Tiller, Terence, *The Inward Animal* (London: Hogarth Press, 1943).

——, *Poems* (London: Hogarth Press, 1941).

——, *Unarm, Eros* (London: Hogarth Press, 1947).

The Times Literary Supplement, 1939–1945.

Tomlinson, Charles, 'The Middlebrow Muse', Review of *New Lines*, *Essays in Criticism*, 7, 2 (April 1957) pp. 208–17.

——, 'Rock Bottom', Review of *Poets of the 1950s*. *Poetry* (Chicago), 89, 4 (January 1957) pp. 260–4.

Treece, Henry, *Herbert Read* (London: Faber & Faber, 1944).

——, *Dylan Thomas* (New York: John de Graff, 1956).

——, *How I See Apocalypse* (London: Lindsay Drummond, 1946).

Twentieth-Century Verse (ed. Julian Symons), 1937–38.

Tymms, Ralph, *Doubles in Literary Psychology* (Cambridge: Bowes, 1949).

Wain, John, 'Ambiguous Gifts', *Penguin New Writing*, 40 (1950) pp. 116–128.

—— (ed.), *Anthology of Contemporary Poetry* (London: Hutchinson, 1979).

—— (ed.), *Anthology of Modern Poetry* (London: Hutchinson, 1963, rep. 1967).

——, 'Engagement or Withdrawal? Some Notes on the Work of Philip Larkin', *Critical Quarterly*, 6, 2 (Summer 1946) pp. 167–78.

——, 'English Poetry: The Immediate Situation', *Sewanee Review*, LXV, 3 (1957) pp. 353–74.

——, *Mixed Feelings* (Reading: University of Reading Fine Art Department, 1951).

——, *Preliminary Essays* (London: Macmillan, 1957).

——, *Sprightly Running* (London: Macmillan, 1962; reprinted with alterations, 1963, 1965).

Waugh, Evelyn, Letter, *Spectator* (8 October 1954) p. 434.

Whitman, Walt, *When Lilacs Last in the Door Yard Bloom'd: Sequel to Drum Taps* (1865–6) (ed. F. DeWolfe Miller) (Florida: Scholars' Facsimiles and Reprints, 1959).

Wind and the Rain (ed. Neville Braybrooke), 1947–49.

The Windmill (eds Reginald Moore and Edward Lane), 1944–8.

Woolf, Virginia, *Between the Acts* (London: Hogarth Press, 1941; New York: Harcourt, Brace, Jovanovich, 1969).

——, 'The Leaning Tower', *Folios of New Writing*, 2 (Autumn 1940) pp. 11–29.

——, 'Rupert Brooke', *TLS* (8 August 1918) p. 371.
——, *A Writer's Diary* (ed. Leonard Woolf) (London: Hogarth Press, 1953; New York: Harcourt Brace Jovanovich, 1954).

II   SECONDARY SOURCES

Allsop, Kenneth, *The Angry Decade* (London: Peter Owen, 1958).
Alvarez, A., 'Back in 1956 and . . .' Interview with Ian Hamilton in Dannie Abse (ed.), *Best Poetry of the Year* 6 (London: Robson Books, 1979) pp. 103–22.
——, 'Beyond the Gentility Principle', in his *Beyond All This Fiddle* (London: Penguin Press, Allen Lane, 1968) pp. 34–44.
——, 'Poetry of the Fifties: in England', in *International Literary Annual* 1 (ed. John Wain) (New York: Criterion, 1959) pp. 97–107.
Aragon, Louis, *Poet of Resurgent France* (eds Hannah Josephson and Malcolm Cowley) (London: Pilot Press, 1946).
Banerjee, A., *Spirit Above Wars* (London: Macmillan, 1976).
Bedient, Calvin, *Eight Contemporary Poets* (New York: Oxford University Press, 1974).
Bergonzi, Bernard, 'After the Movement', *The Listener*, 66 (1961) pp. 284–5.
——, 'Davie, Larkin, and the State of England', *Contemporary Literature*, 18, 3 (Summer 1977) pp. 343–60.
——, *Heroes Twilight* (London: Constable, 1965).
——, *Reading the Thirties; Texts and Contexts* (London: Macmillan, 1978).
——, 'Reputations: Kingsley Amis', *London Magazine*, 3, 10 (January 1964) pp. 50–65.
Berry, Francis, *Herbert Read* (London: Longman, 1953).
Bowen, Roger, 'Native and Exile: The Poetry of Bernard Spencer', *Malahat Review* (January 1979) pp. 5–27.
Bradbury, Malcolm, *The Social Context of Modern English Literature* (Oxford: Basil Blackwell, 1971).
Briggs, Asa, *Sound and Vision, IV. The History of Broadcasting in the United Kingdom* (Oxford: Oxford University Press, 1979).
Brownjohn, Alan, *Philip Larkin* (London: Longman, 1975).
Bullough, Geoffrey, *Mirror of Minds: Changing Psychological Beliefs in English Poetry* (University of London: The Athlone Press, 1962).
——, *The Trend of Modern Poetry* (Edinburgh: Oliver and Boyd, 2nd edn, 1941).
Casey, John, 'Tough', review of *Keith Douglas 1920–1944 The New Review*, I, 5 (August 1974) pp. 73–4.
Cecil, Lord David, and Allen Tate (eds), Introduction to *Modern Verse in English* (London: Eyre and Spottiswoode, 1958).
Calder, Angus, *The People's War, Britain 1939–1945* (New York: Pantheon Books, 1979).
Coleman, Antony, 'T. S. Eliot and Keith Douglas', *TLS* (2 July 1970) p. 731.
'Context', *London Magazine*, NS. 1, 11 (February 1962) pp. 27–53.
Cowley, Malcolm, 'A Note on Literary Generations', in his *And I Worked at the Writer's Trade* (New York: The Viking Press, 1978) pp. 1–20.
Cox, C. B., 'Featuring Philip Larkin', *Critical Quarterly*, 1, 1 (Spring 1959) pp. 14–17.

Currey, R. N., *Poets of the 1939–1945 War* (London: Longman, 1960).

Davidson, Mildred, *The Poetry is in the Pity* (New York: Barnes and Noble, 1972).

Davie, Donald, 'Eliot in One Poet's Life', *Mosaic*, IV, 1 (Fall 1972) pp. 229–41.

——, 'Remembering the Movement'. In his *The Poet in the Imaginary Museum: Essays of Two Decades* (ed. Barry Alpert) (Manchester: Carcanet Press, 1977) pp. 72–5.

——, *Thomas Hardy and British Poetry* (New York: Oxford University Press, 1972).

——, 'The Varsity Match', in Dannie Abse (ed.), *Best Poetry of the Year 3* (London: Robson Books, 1975) pp. 101–13. Originally published in *Poetry Nation*, 2 (1974) pp. 72–80.

Davin, Dan, *Closing Times* (Oxford: Oxford University Press, 1975).

Dickins, Anthony, 'Tambimuttu and *Poetry (London)*', *London Magazine*, V, 9 (1965) pp. 53–7.

Dodsworth, Martin (ed.), *The Survival of Poetry* (London: Faber & Faber, 1970).

Evans, B. Ifor, *English Literature Between the Wars* (London: Methuen, 1948).

Falck, Colin, 'Philip Larkin', in Ian Hamilton (ed.), *The Modern Poet* (London: Macdonald, 1969).

Fedden, Robin, *Personal Landscape* (a history of the magazine) (London: Turret Books, 1966).

Feaver, William, 'The Thirties', *The Listener*, 102 (25 October 1979) pp. 538–40.

Ferguson, Peter, 'Philip Larkin's *XX Poems*: The Missing Link', *Agenda*, XIV, 3 (1976) pp. 53–65.

FitzGibbon, Constantine, *The Life of Dylan Thomas* (Boston: Little Brown, 1965).

Fraser, G. S., Roy Fuller, and others, 'English Poetry since 1945', *London Magazine*, IV, 4 (November 1959) pp. 11–36.

——, *Essays on Twentieth Century Poets* (Leicester: University Press, 1977).

——, *Lawrence Durrell* (London: Longman, 1970).

——, *The Modern Writer and His World* (London: Derek Verschoyle, 1953).

——, 'The Poet and His Medium', in John Lehmann (ed.), *The Craft of Letters in England* (London: The Cresset Press, 1956) pp. 98ff.

——, *Poetry Now* (London: Faber & Faber, 1956).

——, 'A Tribute to Empson', in Dannie Abse (ed.), *Best Poetry of the Year 3* (London: Robson Books, 1975) pp. 13–26.

——, *Vision and Rhetoric: Studies in Modern Poetry* (London: Faber & Faber, 1959).

Fuller, Roy, 'Poetry, Tradition and Belief', in John Lehmann (ed.), *The Craft of Letters in England* (London: The Cresset Press, 1956) pp. 74–82.

Fussell, Paul, *Abroad* (London: Oxford University Press, 1980).

——, *The Great War and Modern Memory* (London: Oxford University Press, 1975).

Gardner, Helen, *The Composition of the Four Quartets* (London: Oxford University Press, 1978).

Glendinning, Victoria, *Elizabeth Bowen* (New York: Avon Books, 1977).

Goode, Stephen, 'British War Poetry of the Second World War', dissertation, University of Pennsylvania, 1958.

Graham, Desmond, *Keith Douglas 1920–1944, A Biography* (Oxford: Oxford University Press, 1974).

Graves, Robert, *Poetic Craft and Principle* (London: Cassell, 1967).

Grubb, Frederick, *A Vision of Reality* (London: Chatto & Windus, 1965).

Guenther, John, *Sidney Keyes* (London: London Magazine Editions, 1967).

Haffenden, John, 'The True and the Beautiful: A Conversation with Philip Larkin', *London Magazine*, 20, 1/2 (April/May 1980) pp. 81–96.

Hall, Donald, 'Interview with T. S. Eliot', *The Paris Review* (Spring/Summer 1959) pp. 47–70.

Hamburger, Michael, *The Truth of Poetry: Tensions in Modern Poetry from Baudelaire to the 1960s* (London: Weidenfeld & Nicolson, 1969).

Hamilton, Ian, 'The Forties', orginally printed in four parts in *London Magazine*, 1965, reprinted in *A Poetry Chronicle* (London: Faber & Faber, 1973) pp. 55–86.

——, 'Four Conversations', *London Magazine*, IV, 8 (November 1964) pp. 64–85.

——, *The Little Magazines, A Study of Six Editors* (London: Weidenfeld & Nicolson, 1976).

——, 'The Making of the Movement', in his *A Poetry Chronicle* (London: Faber & Faber, 1973) pp. 128–33.

——, (ed.), *The Modern Poet: Essays from The Review* (London: MacDonald, 1968).

Hassall, Christopher, *Rupert Brooke: A Biography* (New York: Faber & Faber, 1964).

Helmstadter, T. H., 'The Apocalyptic Movement in British Poetry', dissertation, University of Pennsylvania, 1963.

Hewison, Robert, *Under Siege: Literary Life in London 1939–45* (London: Weidenfeld & Nicolson, 1977).

Hoffman, Frederick J., 'From Surrealism to "The Apocalypse" ', *ELH*, XV (1948) pp. 147–65.

Holbrook, David, *Lost Bearings in English Poetry* (London: Vision Press, 1977).

Homberger, Eric, *The Art of the Real* (London: Dent, 1977).

Hughes, Ted, 'The Poetry of Keith Douglas', *Critical Quarterly*, 5, 1 (Spring 1963) pp. 43–8.

Hynes, Samuel, *The Auden Generation, Literature and Politics in England in the 1930s* (London: Bodley Head, 1976).

——, 'What is a Decade? Notes on the Thirties', *Sewanee Review* (July–Sept. 1980) pp. 506–11.

Jacobson, Dan, 'Profile 3: Philip Larkin', *The New Review*, I, 3 (June 1974) pp. 25–8.

James, Clive, 'Profile 4: Kingsley Amis', *The New Review*, I, 4 (July 1974) pp. 21–9.

Jones, Alun R., 'The Poetry of Philip Larkin: A Note on Transatlantic Culture', *Western Humanities Review*, XVI, 2 (Spring 1962) pp 143–52.

Kalstone, David, *Five Temperaments* (Oxford: Oxford University Press, 1977).

Lehmann, John, *Thrown to the Woolfs* (London: Weidenfeld & Nicolson, 1978).

——, *Virginia Woolf and her World* (London: Thames and Hudson, 1975).

Litz, A. Walton, 'Revising the Thirties', *Sewanee Review*, LXXXVII, 4 (Fall 1979) pp. 660–6.

Lodge, David, 'The Modern, The Contemporary and the Importance of Being Amis', *Critical Quarterly*, V, 4 (Winter 1963) pp. 335–54.

Martin, Bruce, *Philip Larkin* (Boston: Twayne, 1978).

Maud, R. N., *Entrances to Dylan Thomas' Poetry* (Pittsburgh: University of Pittsburgh Press, 1963).

——, *Poet in the Making* (London: Dent, 1968).

Mellors, John, 'Dreams in War: Second Thoughts on Elizabeth Bowen', *London Magazine*, 19, 8 (November 1979) pp. 64–9.

Meyer, Michael, 'John Heath-Stubbs in the Forties', in Dannie Abse (ed.), *Best Poetry of the Year 6* (London: Robson Books, 1979) pp. 179–87.

Miles, Josephine, *The Primary Language of Poetry in the 1940s* (Berkeley: University of California Press, 1948).

Miller, Karl (ed.), *Writing in England Today, The Last Fifteen Years* (Harmondsworth: Penguin, 1968).

Morrison, Blake, *The Movement, English Poetry and Fiction of the 1950s* (Oxford: Oxford University Press, 1980).

Muggeridge, Malcolm, *The Thirties: 1930–1940 in Great Britain* (London: Collins, 1964; originally Hamish Hamilton, 1940).

'The 1940s', *The Cherwell*, 11 November 1970, pp. 7–12.

O'Connor, William Van, *The New University Wits* (Carbondale: Southern Illinois University Press, 1963).

Orr, Peter (ed.), *The Poet Speaks* (London: Routledge & Kegan Paul, 1966).

Partridge, A. C., *The Language of Poetry* (London: André Deutsch, 1976).

Perkins, David, *A History of Modern Poetry from the 1890s to the High Modernist Mode* (Cambridge, Mass.: Harvard University Press, 1976).

'Poetry Since the War: A Symposium', *London Magazine*, 5, 11 (November 1959) pp. 11–36.

Porter, Peter, 'Auden's Profession', in Dannie Abse (ed.), *Best Poetry of the Year 6* (London: Robson Books, 1979) pp. 23–30.

Press, John, *A Map of Modern English Verse* (New York: Oxford University Press, 1969).

——, *Rule and Energy* (Oxford: Oxford University Press, 1963).

Pritchard, William, *Seeing Through Everything, 1918–1940* (New York: Oxford University Press, 1977).

Prochaska, Alice, *Young Writers of the Thirties* (London: National Portrait Gallery Publications, 1976).

Rajiva, Stanley, 'The Appearance of Choice: A Critical Examination of Themes and Attitudes in English Poetry of the Second World War', dissertation, University of Wisconsin, 1967.

Rank, Otto, *The Double* (tr. and ed. Harry Tucker, Jr.) (New York: New American Library, 1971; originally published 1925).

Raper, Michell, 'Fitzrovia and the War', *The Listener* (3 October 1974) pp. 428–9.

Ray, Paul C., *The Surrealist Movement in England* (Ithaca: Cornell University Press, 1971).

Roberts, Michael (ed.), *The Faber Book of Modern Verse* (supp. by Anne Ridler) (London: Faber & Faber, 1957).

Rodway, Allan, 'A Note on Contemporary English Poetry', *Texas Quarterly*, 4, 3 (Autumn 1961) pp. 66–72.

Rosenthal, M. L., *The Modern Poets, A Critical Introduction* (New York: Oxford University Press, 1960).

——, *The New Poets: American and British Poetry Since World War II* (New York: Oxford University Press, 1967).

Ross, Alan, 'The Poetry of Keith Douglas', *TLS* (6 August 1954) pp. xxii.

Ross, R. H., *The Georgian Revolt* (Carbondale: Southern Illinois University Press, 1965).

Sale, Roger, 'England's Parnassus', *Hudson Review*, XVII, 2 (Summer 1964) pp. 203–25.

Salmon, Arthur, Edward, *Poets of the Apocalypse* (Boston: Twayne, 1983).

Scannell, Vernon, *Not Without Glory: Poets of the Second World War* (London: Woburn Press, 1976).

Schorske, Carl, *Fin de Siècle Vienna* (New York: Knopf, 1979).

Sergeant, Howard, 'The Movement – An Agreed Fiction?' in Dannie Abse (ed.), *Best Poetry of the Year 6* (London: Robson Books, 1979) pp. 123–36.

—— (ed.), *Poetry of the 1940s* (London: Longman, 1970).

Silkin, Jon, *Out of Battle* (Oxford: Oxford University Press, 1972).

——, 'Triumphant Silence: Some Aspects of Sidney Keyes, 1922–1943', *London Magazine*, 20, 1/2 (April/May 1980) pp. 120–6.

Sisson, C. H., *English Poetry 1900–1950, An Assessment* (London: Rupert Hart-Davis, 1971).

Skelton, Robin, *Poetic Truth* (London: Heinemann, 1978).

Spears, Monroe K., *Dionysus and the City, Modernism in Twentieth Century Poetry* (New York: Oxford University Press, 1970).

Spender, Stephen, *The Struggle of the Modern* (Berkeley: University of California Press, 1963).

——, *The Thirties and After* (New York: Vintage Books, 1979).

Spitzer, Alan B., 'The Historical Problem of Generations', *The American Historical Review*, 78, 5 (December 1973) pp. 1354ff.

Stanford, Derek, *Movements in English Poetry, 1900–1958* (London: Centaur Press Reprint, 1958).

Symons, Julian, *The Detective Story in Britain* (London: Longman, 1962).

——, *The Thirties, A Dream Revolved* (London: Faber & Faber, 1960; rev. 1975).

Thwaite, Anthony, *Contemporary English Poetry, An Introduction* (London: Heinemann, 1957; 1959).

——, *Twentieth Century English Poetry* (London: Heinemann, 1978).

Tolley, A. T., *The Poetry of the Thirties* (Edinburgh: Oliver and Boyd, 1973; London: Victor Gollancz, 1975).

Tomlinson, Charles, 'Poetry To-day', in Boris Ford (ed.), *The Pelican Guide to English Literature, VII: The Modern Age* (Harmondsworth: Penguin, 1961) pp. 458–74.

——, *Some Americans: A Personal Record* (Berkeley: University of California, 1980).

Walsh, Chad, 'The Postwar Revolt in England Against "Modern Poetry!"', *Bucknell Review*, XIII, 3 (1965) pp. 97–105.

Williams, John Stuart, 'The Poetry of Alun Lewis', *The Anglo-Welsh Review*, 14, 33 (1964) pp. 59–70.

Williams, Oscar (ed.), introduction, *The War Poets* (New York: Day and Co., 1945).

Wohl, Robert, *The Generation of 1914* (Cambridge: Harvard University Press, 1979).

'The Writer in His Age', a symposium, *London Magazine*, 4, 5 (May 1957) pp. 38–55.

Ziolkowski, Theodore, 'The Literature of Atrocity', *Sewanee Review*, LXXXV (January–March 1977) pp. 135–44.

Zwerdling, Alex, *Orwell and the Left* (New Haven: Yale University Press, 1974).

Index

169